Your Career,
Your Responsibility

The road map to internship and early career success

You have what it takes

Uche.

Uche Ezichi

About The Author

Uche Ezichi is a speaker and coach, with a focus on leadership and career development. He works with global organisations to develop their leaders and is a preferred coach with top business schools including INSEAD, Imperial College Business School and Barcelona's IESE Business School. He works with their MBA and Executive MBA students, coaching them in their pursuit of new roles or helping them make the transition into more senior leadership positions. He has worked as an Investment Banker and held various Talent Management and Recruitment positions in organisations such as Goldman Sachs and Morgan Stanley.

He runs his own private coaching practice, working with clients from around the world.

Your Career,
Your Responsibility

Copyright © Uche Ezichi 2017

ISBN: 978-1541246041

Published by Aceeva Consulting Ltd

Printed in United Kingdom

Amazon Reviews

Everyone needs to grab a copy

I need everyone to just get a copy of this book it is truly a life changer. It changes the way you think and gives you a winning approach towards the whole application process. This morning as soon as I woke up I continued reading this book to get fired up for the day. The tips and words of wisdom in this book will help you get that internship or job offer you require. The author is so relatable and all his points are clear and concise with loads of examples to show you how you can implement them in your own life and also he highlights deal breakers in the application process. I mean as long as you need a job now or will need one in the future you will forever need this book. It also helps that the author has a good sense of humor which makes this book a great read....

*Amazon Reviewer 1*****

Good read, great foundation

This book has very good advice for mostly students who want to start a career in any industry. The examples given are of careers in the corporate setting (i.e. Bankers, Lawyers etc) however the advice can be applied else where. It is very inspirational as it offers words of encouragement to those who might not have good grades. Ultimately the key message is confidence in your ability.

*Amazon Reviewer 2****

Simply Brilliant!

This book is a MUST READ for anyone serious about maximizing their potential and getting the best out of their career. For a debut piece of work, the author has succeeded in producing one of the most realistic and comprehensive career guides of our time. This is clearly an author whose work I eagerly anticipate to read more of in the future. I only wish the book was written a lot earlier in my career. Perhaps I would have avoided some of the mistakes I made. However, the beauty of 'Your career, your responsibility', is that Uche manages to produce a book that applies across many career stages. It applies to the bright-eyed intern as much as it does to the high-flying CEO. It truly is timeless material. Get your copy now and avoid any further mistakes on your chosen career path.

Amazon Reviewer 3

"The truth the whole truth and nothing but the truth"

The book takes the reader through everything from the fundamental errors people make as early as application stage to the longer term career goals those hoping for success should set themselves. The book is therefore a must read not only for those embarking on or attempting to secure internships/early work experience as part of university studies (which has become so paramount in today's job market) but equally relevant to those already through the first hurdle and embarking on full-time employment looking for that extra motivation/courage to chase their end game career dreams. Also serves as a great pick-me-up for any recent career setbacks the reader may have experienced as there is true empathy with the writer whilst he shares the not so smooth road that lead him to where he is today.

I found it a very accessible and easy to follow book. The main messages are clearly defined and the ongoing story lines within the book help sustain interest. The writer draws on personal experiences using both himself and four main character references so that the reader has an array of real life experiences to relate to.

Amazon Reviewer 4****

Inspiring

As the author promised in the beginning, the book contains so many words of advice scattered all through. It is a must read for all students, especially university students. I particularly like the message that the author conveyed; YOU play a major role in determining your future. It has made me want more out of life and dream without limits.

*Amazon Reviewer 5*****

Thought provoking and brilliant book...foundation for success!

As a student approaching my final year, this book has arrived at a crucial time for me. It has helped me highlight what I need to do and the steps I need to take, in order to elevate myself to the next level. The author clearly depicts the trials and setbacks we all may face, but offers excellent advice and tools we can adopt in order to counteract this. It's an easy, but thought provoking read. The book is not limited to just one career route; it covers a multitude and takes into account the different starting points individuals in society face. In addition the author donates his experience and tips for securing great interviews and better yet keeping the job. The book is exceptional in the way, real life people and scenarios are used, thus allowing the reader to connect. I sincerely look forward to the next installment. I dare anyone to read this book and not be challenged to do better. The first step in achieving your success is simple.... BUY THIS BOOK.

*Amazon reviewer 6*****

Very well written and useful book

I really enjoyed this book. I literally read about three quarters of the book in one sitting. I love how the author uses real life people - some of whom we all recognise in our day to day lives and uses this to show very important career mistakes and successes. Whilst I sometimes feel that I am a bit long in the tooth with my career, this book certainly made me do a stock check on what I thought I knew and re-teach myself about those fundamental behaviours that we sometimes all forget. Much enjoyed and I look forward to the next installment.

Amazon reviewer 7*****

Simply Brilliant!

This book is a MUST READ for anyone serious about maximizing their potential and getting the best out of their career. For a debut piece of work, the author has succeeded in producing one of the most realistic and comprehensive career guides of our time. This is clearly an author whose work I eagerly anticipate to read more of in the future. I only wish the book was written a lot earlier in my career. Perhaps I would have avoided some of the mistakes I made. However, the beauty of 'Your career, your responsibility', is that Uche manages to produce a book that applies across many career stages. It applies to the bright-eyed intern as much as it does to the high-flying CEO. It truly is timeless material. Get your copy now and avoid any further mistakes on your chosen career path.

Amazon reviewer 8 ****

Book you can't put down!!!

I learnt a lot from this book, it was really inspiring. As a young professional about to start my career I got many useful tips on networking, improving confidence, being innovative at the work place, how to be successful in my job and always aiming high. Surprisingly, it was also a funny read!!! Thoroughly interesting - I would recommend this book to anyone about to begin their internship or at the start of their professional career.

Amazon Reviewer 9*****

Dedication

To my parents for believing in me.

To Vona my sweetie, my biggest fan and critic;

your support and encouragement made this book a reality.

Contents

Note to the Reader

After years of working in the City[1], I now know how wrong my opinion was about people who succeed. When I was at university, I thought that one needed to be a prodigy or have certain grooming i.e. private schooling and a top-10 university education, in order to get into the City and succeed. To my surprise, nothing could be further from the truth. Definitely, educational excellence helps but I have seen students with less than average educational backgrounds succeed in the City where students with stellar backgrounds failed to get in. Intrigued by this discovery, I started thinking long and hard about why this was the case. My conclusion was that success depends on the individual and not their credentials. If this is true, then there must be attributes that distinguish successful students from unsuccessful ones.

Nowadays, an internship is the primary way that most organisations recruit for their graduate programmes. It is important to bear in mind that, even as a graduate starting your career, you will usually be on a two-year contract, so you are, in effect, on an extended internship. Therefore, my use of the word 'internship' is not restricted to that six- to ten-week-long programme that you complete in summer. In my opinion, you should still consider yourself an intern even in the first few years as a graduate trainee because having an intern mentality – the eagerness to learn, the enthusiasm to work and the desperation to prove yourself in the limited time that you have, would serve you well to succeed early in your career.

Using my own journey as a case study, I would like to share with you the path that led me to a position in the investment-banking arm of one of the world's largest banks. At that time (like now), getting into banking was no walk in the park as there was a boom and most graduates wanted to work in an investment

---

[1] The 'City' is the term used to describe the major business and financial centre in London. It is the home of a wide range of institutions, such as law firms, banks, insurers and professional services firms. I use the term for convenience and because it encompasses the majority of professions sought after by students. However, the principles in this book remain relevant even if you aspire for a career outside the City.

bank. However, over time, my passion for helping people became evident to me and those I worked with. As I chased after my passion, I started working in the Leadership and Diversity team at a top-tier international investment bank, helping individuals like you, achieve their potential.

We live in a time where your success has little to do with your gender, race, height or weight. We live in a time where it is up to you and nobody else to write your own story; a time where it is up to you to become all you ever dreamed and more. As I cast my mind back to when I was a student before starting my career, I find myself saying, "If only I knew then what I know now, I would have gone much further." I do not claim to know it all, but I certainly know a lot about what it takes to succeed. These tried, tested and proven principles that I share in this book are not just for aspiring bankers.

So, what leads to success? If that is the question you are asking, then you have the right book in your hands. In this book, I have delineated the key principles of success, the application of which would greatly increase your chances of getting an internship or full-time offer in your chosen industry. The key is application. You may know the steps to digging for diamonds, and you may even know where the diamonds are, but if you don't get down there and start digging, you won't become rich.

The principles shared in this book will help everybody, regardless of their career path or industry. By the end of the book, you will have a clear idea of what practical steps you can take to increase your chances of success. A word of caution, though – the success principles I share are scattered throughout this book, from the first page to the last. There is no section titled 'Key Success Principles', so please read attentively, carefully seeking for gems on each page and making notes of those points that you never want to forget. Most importantly, what you learn, put it into action immediately, because the information you receive, no matter how valuable, becomes worthless if you don't act on it. I can guarantee you will come back to this book many times as a reference.

Only you can stop you!

Chapter 1
It's Possible

Introduction

When I was young, like most kids my career aspirations were constantly changing from being a superhero to a lawyer and then a teacher, but just before I finished O Levels at age 16, I met a guy called Ike who basically changed the way I dreamed. Everything about him was attractive – the way he dressed, the car he drove, his confidence, all did it for me. He was clearly living the good life, and when my sister told me he was a banker, that was it – I was going to become a banker too.

Is It Really Happening?

One night, nine years later, I was almost too excited to go to bed. The following morning, I would be hanging out in Bedford with company executives, bank managing directors and law firm partners at the Palmer Autodrome to drive a selection of some of the world's greatest high-performance cars and I was nervous. The closest I had come to a Formula-1 car was seeing Hamilton turbo down the racetracks on TV, but that was about to change. As I stepped out of my house that next morning, a black BMW 7 series with tinted windows pulled up – it was my cab. I sunk into the owner's corner and thanked God for the day I met Ike, the day I decided I wanted to be a banker. That ride to King's Cross Station was absolute bliss. I stared out the tinted windows and thought: "How does a 25-year-old get to this point?" Certainly, some element of luck, but the major factor was a decision to work hard at fulfilling a dream of becoming a banker – what is your dream?

In Bedford at the Palmer Autodrome, all of us, mostly law firm partners, company executives, bank managing directors and associates like me, could hardly remain in our seats. We were excited as the instructor talked through the line-up of cars we would be driving on the different race courses. At the end of the day, none of us could hide our excitement. As we sat there enjoying some nibbles and talking about the best and the worst drivers for each race, I remembered how, only three years before, I was eagerly trying to network with bankers at recruitment events and how my friends and I would gather around the table and dream of heading to work in the City. Now, here I was, having some down time with company executives, and just the day before, I was working on multi-million-pound transactions, managing multiple projects, having a series of conference calls and earning much more than the average person.

I started thinking about how it was all worth it, all the hard work had paid off – the discipline of daily reading to prepare for interviews, practicing all those numeracy tests and having those prep interviews. As my thoughts came back to the present, I looked around the tables. Although some of these people went to different universities in the top-10 bracket, a good proportion of the individuals around me had attended what society deems as "OK" universities, which really drove home the fact that it is up to the individual to succeed. We all shared certain attributes – we were all driven, focused and hardworking. I know this because of the hours we had put into trying to execute transactions. As I headed home, reminiscing on the day, I felt like taking the next day off and heading to universities and shouting from the rooftops, "You can do it!" "You can live your dream! You can get a job in the City or anywhere else! Don't give up, keep pushing, and you will succeed!"

My Background

What you may find most interesting is the twist in my background! From what you have read so far, you might assume that I went to a top university, got all A's in A Levels, A*'s in my O Levels and went to a private school. Well, apart from going to a top university (University of Bristol), I did not meet the other criteria. I attended a state secondary school in Lagos, Nigeria, and my performance was mediocre. For instance, in my final junior secondary school exams (the equivalent of the old year 9 SATs in the UK), I had five C's and seven P's, which is equivalent of grades C's and D's. In year 8, I was promoted on trial to year 9, i.e. I had the first term to prove that I should remain in year 9, or repeat the year. I went to a private sixth-form college in London that, unknown to my dad, had poor academic and teaching standards. I didn't have the luxury of being surrounded by smart kids to keep me on my toes and push me to perform. In spite of this, I worked hard and made it into Bristol with an 'A' in Math, 'B' in Economics and 'C' in Politics. My background was not one of a star student from Eton or the like, but I did not let my record from the past affect my future. I learnt from my mistakes and decided to work hard. The fact that I got three B's and five C's in my O Levels and attended a state school didn't prevent me from getting into Bristol. Getting into Bristol back then was akin to getting into the City, and neither my O Levels nor my A Levels was an A* performance. The point I am trying to make is this – it was up to me as an individual to fulfil my dream of getting into the City regardless of what university I attended or what grades I got. Academic excellence certainly helps, but your future success depends on more than attending a good university and getting good grades. I am sharing all this to give you a clear picture of where I am coming from and to illustrate that if I can get into the City and excel (I experienced an accelerated career growth), then you certainly can in whatever career you choose.

Here is my solemn declaration on this cause – I promise to tell the truth, the whole truth and nothing but the truth. The fact is, getting in is not as difficult as people make it seem. During my university years, getting a job seemed like trying to climb Everest. In hindsight, after having worked a few years, I began wondering why I had been so scared, and I realised that I had been programmed to think it would be difficult. Often, when I was out with friends, we would joke that we certainly never needed to go through the pain of university to do this job, though I think we all appreciated that education was necessary for our personal development. In fact, I concluded that a degree was just another criterion added to the screening process to assess an individual's ability to commit to a goal and achieve it. Provided you can write, understand basic math, and are willing to learn and work hard, you will be just fine in any industry. So, you must begin to erase all the myths of how difficult it will be to get your dream job from your mind, and embrace the truth that you have what it takes (provided that you apply yourself).

During my years working in the industry, I have learned that it isn't always the stereotypical straight-A student who finishes with a first-class degree that gets the job. Again, don't get me wrong – academic excellence is very good. I saw the light, started to work hard and progressed from barely passing O Levels to getting into Bristol, and by the end of my first year, I was predicted a 2.1, which helped me to obtain my internship. Success in an internship depends on more than academia. Indeed, Napoleon Hill, put it well when he said, "The graduate who has been active on the campus, whose personality is such that he or she gets along with all kinds of people and who has done an adequate job with studies has a most decided edge over the strictly academic student." What employers look for is a rough diamond, one they can cut and polish and that will become very valuable when sold, i.e. your services being provided to the clients. I know you are a diamond, for we all have that innate potential, but the issue is how do you show it and achieve your success. STOP! Recite to yourself: "I am a rough diamond waiting to be discovered and cut into a fine piece!" Say this louder, louder, and louder until you start believing it! If, as Kenneth Hagin, a renowned speaker says, you do not want to live on "Barely Get Along Street, right at the junction of Grumble Alley" for the rest of your life, then please turn the page and let's begin.

The Awesome Four: Ways To The Top

I find it interesting to note how successful students tend to share the same fundamental characteristics yet travel along different paths towards their successes. I will tell the stories of how four people succeeded. For now, I will simply introduce them and summarise their backgrounds. Fatima is the accountant, Leke is the consultant, Steve is the banker and Matilda is the lawyer.

I enjoy making fun of Leke because he and I are opposites. I talk a lot, he says little. I am a loud extrovert, and he is a quiet introvert – it is still a wonder how we ended up being such close friends. Whereas I played O Levels away and only started waking up in A Levels, Leke aced his O Levels with A*'s and A's, and decided that A Levels was the time to chill out. As a result, he ended up with a B, B and C in Math, Electronics and Physics respectively. He still claims that his papers were marked incorrectly, but nonetheless, he got into his choice of university and ultimately studied Computer Systems Engineering.

Fatima was a mummy's girl and probably still is. She is shy, softly spoken and quite emotional. Fatima's the sort that needs boxes of tissues when watching sad movies and who was told *ad nauseum* that she didn't have what it takes to excel in the City. She shares the same priorities as Leke, acing O Levels then ending up with a B, C and C in Business Studies, Information Technology and Sociology, respectively, in her A Levels exams. At university, she studied Business Management.

Matilda is easily one of the most polite and caring people that I know. She always moans at me for not staying in touch. She is reserved, and I like to describe her as "silent but deadly" when it comes to going for her goal. Unlike Leke, who went to a state school, Matilda was privately schooled, and whilst her O Levels weren't particularly encouraging, she made amends during A Levels and finished with two A's and two B's and went on to study law.

Steve is an African immigrant who confesses that he still has gaps in his knowledge because of the very poor educational standards in his O Levels days. He recalls his shock when teachers in his secondary school went on strike because they were not being paid properly. As such, for almost two years, he had to teach himself some subjects while being assisted by students that were more senior. His success in A Levels is very telling of the sort of drive that he has. Coming to study in the UK was a great opportunity that he was going to maximise and although he went to a state school with a poor record, Steve was determined to succeed. After all, poor standards in the UK were still relatively high in comparison to the standards from which he came. When he joined the school, he asked for the university league tables. He highlighted the top five universities and asked what grades he needed to get in. Finishing with one A and two B's, he achieved his goal of going to a top 10 university to study Biochemistry.

Prologue: Laying The Right Foundation

If I took a poll of students in any university asking if they wanted to be successful, I'm certain that 100% of the students would enthusiastically say, "Yes!" Similarly, if asked what 'success' was, most students would probably describe a point in the future when they would have a particular job, a certain amount of money and would be living in their dream house. Such a definition implies that the average individual who has not attained these goals is a failure. Obviously, this cannot be true, and as I pondered what best describes 'success', I remembered a quote that said, "You don't have to be great to start, but you have to start to be great." Success begins when you make that decision to maximise your potential and take the first step.

When I say 'success', I do not mean winning the lottery (winners often end up being broke again), but rather success achieved through hard work and drive. American author Zig Ziglar, put it well when he said, "Success is a process not an event." Like most students, I had a very myopic view of life.

My goal was to get a graduate job and pay my bills. Yet, true success in any career is more than just planning to get a graduate job. A few other factors are essential for achieving true success. While I was at university, I did not know these things. Looking back, I wish I did because it would have put me ahead of my peers. However, I know only a few are willing to pay the price that success requires.

The first factor I will discuss is hard work. "The shortest distance between you and success is hard work." There are simply no short cuts to success. While I was an undergraduate, I quickly embraced this truth and decided to 'take the bull by the horns' by working hard. I was not going to become one of those people who feel like victims because life has not been fair. If you are going to succeed, you must learn to take responsibility for yourself and what happens to you. If you take responsibility for everything that happens to you, then your life will change for good. Sometimes, people mess us up, but anyone who constantly blames others for their own lack of success will never succeed. It is not the interviewer's fault, it isn't human resources' fault, neither is it your parents' fault – it's all up to you. However, hard work is only one element of the success equation. The decision to work hard coupled with a few other attributes will brings you the success you want.

Vision

Very successful people have a vision. Napoleon Hill said, "All success in your life begins with definitiveness of purpose with a clear picture of what you want in your life." Successful people have a clear picture of where they are going. The route might occasionally deviate from the initial plan, but the destination remains fixed. Despite obstacles, persistent people continually push towards their vision. That vision is so real, so captivating, that it becomes like a strong magnetic force drawing them in that direction. Having a vision is a precondition for success in any sphere of life, be it banking, law, consultancy, music, sports, or politics. Often, coaches make their athletes visualise stepping up to the podium, having flowers handed to them and a gold medal being lifted over their bowed heads. It is that vision of crossing the finish line first that encourages athletes to push until the end. Do you have a vision like that? Is there a finish line you are heading for? Is your vision worth the required sacrifices you will have to make?

I remember the day I realised that, with each day that passes, I am one day closer to death. We have no control over the rising and setting of the sun, marking the beginning and end of each day. The good news is that we have the power to maximise our days and ultimately control how we will be remembered. So, I ask again, do you have a vision and is your vision worth the required sacrifices you will have to make? We must take a walk down memory lane and learn from when we were toddlers. We all had dreams – we were going to be superheroes. I once said to my brother "I'll be Superman, you be Batman." Those were the good old days when everything was possible. Then we grew up and out went the dreams – the dreams from which comes vision. Imagine your inner child imploring you to dream again, to dream big and to begin creating a vision for your life. Cast off all restraints, all limits, and begin to dream. Tiger Woods' dream was to become the number-one golfer. For Barrack Obama, the dream was to be President of the United States of America. For Sir John Bond, it was becoming the chairman of HSBC. For Ben Carson, it was becoming the number-one brain surgeon in the world. For Bill Gates, it was having the Windows software on every PC in the world. What's important is to note that for each of these people; it all began with a thought, then a dream, and then a vision i.e. a destination.

What I find scary, is the fact that just as a thought was the beginning of these successful people's greatness, likewise, a thought is the beginning of the failure we see in others. The importance of a vision is summarised by Yogi Berra, who said, "You have got to be very careful if you don't know where you are going, because you might not get there." In other words, if you don't have a clear picture of where you're heading, then you're heading nowhere. You run the risk of being like those who underachieve because they don't take time to think about where they're going and how they're going to get there. This is dangerous.

Joel Barker said, "Vision without action is merely a dream. Action without vision just passes the time. Vision with action can change the world!" Over time, I have come to appreciate it when older folks say, "I always knew he would be successful," because I found myself saying the same thing in my final year of university after meeting a first-year student in the Economics library who clearly exemplified turning a dream into vision by taking action. As I was on my way out, this young guy eagerly combing through the pages of the *Financial Times* (FT) caught my attention. I went over, introduced myself, and we got chatting. His name was Matthew, and his enthusiasm was contagious. I started to get excited about joining HSBC at the end of my final year. He explained how he devoted time each day to reading the FT and other websites to gain knowledge about banking and finance. His eyes literally lit up when I explained I had just finished an internship and was offered a graduate position. He eagerly wanted to learn about my experience and shared his vivid vision of joining the industry, becoming a very successful banker and ultimately founding his own firm.

I was surprised at the clarity of his vision, and a little intimidated. I mean, here I was on top of the world because I had an offer and here was this first-year student talking about a level of success I had thought was reserved for superstars (something I had never dreamt of – at least certainly not in my first year). Hoping to know more, I asked how he intended to go about doing this. Many people are all talk but no action, with big aspirations but no substance. Some haven't taken the time to think about how it will all happen and thus they have no idea as to how they are going to turn their dreams into reality. If you meet these people again years later, they are still dreaming and saying, "One day, my dream will come true." This guy wasn't one of those dreamers. He had a plan, and to my surprise, he took me on a clearly mapped-out journey.

He said the first thing he was setting out to do was to know everything he could about the industry (which is constantly changing). He planned to do a spring internship during his first year, and in the summer, get some work experience in the industry. After his second year, he planned to do an internship and receive an offer. After his analyst or graduate programme, he said, he would decide if it would be the right time to get a Master's in Business Administration (MBA). By the time he was through, I thought, "This fellow is going to be very successful, and I must stay in touch with him."

One thing that stood out to me was the fact that, while other students spoke about trying to get an internship or an offer, he was confident that he would make it happen. He believed in himself and his ability. True to form, he did his spring internship, gained work experience, did a summer internship (through the prestigious Sponsors for Educational Opportunities (SEO)) and received a full-time offer. Again, we see the recipe for success here – he had a clear picture of what he wanted, believed he could do it, worked hard and is now living his dream.

Many graduates straight out of university want a job for two main reasons. Firstly, because it is what is expected and secondly, because they need to pay bills and pass the time. They have the action part sorted out but for what purpose and for what vision? In the City, I've seen 40- to 50-year-olds reporting to higher-ups who are 30- to 35-years-old, which proves Ed Cole's observation that "Men without an organised system of thought will always be at the mercy of men who have one." An organised system of thought simply means having a vision and a plan of how to get there. If you aim at nothing, you will hit it. A job is good, but it is not enough. We are talking here about your success and legacy; it is how clearly you envisage the top that keeps you motivated until you get there. Otherwise, you run the risk of working for the rest of your life to pay bills and a mortgage, only to end up with a pension. I can easily recall ten individuals who fall into this category. I remember them grumbling their way through the day, and I'm sure they wished they could turn back time and make changes, although they won't admit it.

I believe that if you are reading this book you are someone who wants to be successful and become an influential force to be reckoned with. You may not have a clear vision right now, and that's okay – all of us, at some point, had no vision. However, it is important to start setting aside time to dream and start envisioning the success that you want – and that you will eventually become. The more you take time to dream and envision, the more attractive the future will become and the more motivation you will need to make it a reality. Remember that, in any field, a leader isn't a leader because he has a vision; rather, it is the vision that eventually makes the person a leader.

Belief

The second attribute of very successful people is belief. The most important thing to note is that belief in yourself and your dream, or lack thereof, becomes a self-fulfilling prophecy. What you believe will come to pass. Successful people believe that what they have envisioned is possible. Unlike the vast population that live in mediocrity, the belief system of these successful people isn't a casual belief that their vision may or may not happen. Neither is it a que será será belief that says, "Whatever will be will be," or the false belief that our destinies are really up to fate and out of our control. No, it is the "I will" belief system, like that of Matthew whom I mentioned earlier that says, "Not only is my dream or vision possible, but I will achieve it, and I will continue to work at it as long as I have life in me." Successful people understand that this approach will work eventually. In our generation, we have real-life examples of people who have gone on to achieve phenomenal heights in their fields against all odds, so no one really has any basis or excuse for failing. In my dictionary, nothing is impossible except failure. A task is only impossible until it is achieved. On a daily basis, in our routine activities, we rely on what was once impossible. Once upon a time, there were no airplanes. Then, the Wright brothers envisioned men flying, believed it was possible and experimented persistently until they made it happen. Therefore, having a dream or a vision isn't enough – you must believe, beyond all doubt, that it is POSSIBLE and that YOU will achieve it.

Many people have no trouble with believing, but their stumbling block is that their vision is too small. Dreaming is free my friends, therefore, if you are going to dream, dream big. While some have a vision of eradicating poverty, others have a vision of paying off a mortgage. My motto is to aim high and have success as my fall back, so it is either success or success in the end. Either way, I am clear on one thing, I will succeed. If you envision being a CEO and you fall short of achieving that position, you could earn a position as the Managing Director of a division instead.

The importance of holding a vision and strong belief was summarised by Napoleon Hill, who said, "Whatever the mind of a man can conceive and believe, it can achieve." To conceive means to imagine, to envision, to visualise, to picture. Therefore, if you can conceive it and believe it, then there is nothing stopping you. Nevertheless, it is important to notice that he said a mind that has conceived and believed, "CAN achieve" and not "WILL achieve." This is like Newton's first law of motion, "All objects remain at a state of rest until a force is applied." In other words, nothing happens until you take ACTION. I was recently speaking to a friend and sharing a few ideas I was very excited about, and as I was about to get off the phone, he said something profound that has remained with me ever since. He said, "Uche, I want you to remember one thing – 'Action beats inaction'." In essence, we all dream, but only a few turn their dreams into reality. Dreaming is good, but it is action that brings reward; it is action that transforms our dreams into realities. This goes for anyone – from the author to the professional to the business owner. Therefore, dream, think and plan, but don't stop there – take action.

Determination

The third attribute necessary is determination, for "there is power in a made-up mind," says Sam Adeyemi, an author and speaker. Determination is the decision that you make, even before you start, that no matter what, you aren't going to give up. When you say no matter what the obstacle, no matter how difficult it gets, you will see it through to the end. Such determination is possible, you only have to completely believe that you can and will achieve what you set out to do. Success comes from your ability to stick with it through the storms. Being determined gets difficult if you are not patient, though, so you must wait for your hard work to start paying off. Too many people are impatient and give up, not realising that the hour is darkest just before dawn.

One of the best examples of determination I have seen was in the movie *Slumdog Millionaire*. As a kid, Salim, idolised a musician and dreamed (had a vision) of seeing his idol one day and getting his autograph. He even carried around a photograph of this musician so that he would be prepared when the opportunity came. As expected, the opportunity did arrive, but as the star's helicopter touched down in the small village, his mischievous older brother locked him in the toilet. Salim had two choices – either miss the opportunity of a lifetime or jump into the pile of human waste below to escape and get his autograph. Like any truly successful person, he wasn't going to let anything get in his way, and he went with option two and ultimately fulfilled his childhood dream. Now that is what I call determination, doing what it takes and overcoming every obstacle to achieve a dream.

Whilst there is a myriad of examples to choose from, one person that I believe encapsulates the word 'greatness' and possesses these attributes in great measure is Nelson Mandela. Here is a man who had a vision to see an end to apartheid, to see a united South Africa, and to become the first black leader of the new regime. I heard the most inspirational story about how he decided in his heart that he had to be mentally sharp and physically fit in order to lead the nation when he finally got out of prison. Remaining mentally sharp was feasible since he was allowed books and writing material in prison; however, being physically fit would prove tough since he spent most of his time in solitary confinement. To keep fit, he jogged in place for close to four hours a day. His vision, belief and determination kept him alive for 27 years in prison, and he eventually achieved his goal. Yes, it is true that we may face unexpected obstacles along the way, but we should be grateful that we don't have to overcome a hurdle of 27 years in prison!

Where you end up ultimately depends on your vision (or lack thereof), whether or not you truly believe it, and if you are willing to work hard and are determined to continue until you achieve it. It is good to be happy with what you have, but don't be content with mediocrity. I challenge you to decide today to rise up and be a voice in your field and in your generation. Now is the time, not tomorrow. You need to realise that a great future awaits you, and it is up to you and no one else to maximise your potential and bring this future to fruition. Enjoy the journey!

Follow Your Passion

Whilst on route to your vision, it is important that you enjoy yourself, for what is life without fun? However, fun only really happens if you do something you are passionate about. Don't let money be your motivation or over time you will burn out and end up depressed, wishing you had followed your passion. People often naively trade in their passion in pursuit of money, failing to realise that if they possess the attributes described above, their passion would eventually bring them all the money they want and more. Some people have been trained to only assess opportunities based on how much money they will bring in. If you fall in to this category and are uncertain about what that passion of yours is, then simply think about the following questions and you will arrive at the vital answer:

1. If money wasn't an issue (i.e. if you had all the money you wanted),

but you still wanted to work, what would you do for free?

2. If all jobs paid exactly the same salary, so that you earned the same whether you were a banker, teacher or a physiotherapist, what line of work would you choose?

Don't be in a rush to answer these questions, take time and honestly assess what you really want to do, which is, in effect, what you were born to do. Otherwise, you might end up chasing the wrong vision and not being fulfilled. Start early doing what you love.

In my career, I almost fell into the wrong category. When I left university, I had a clear vision – I was going to be the CEO of whatever bank I joined. I believed it and was determined to make it happen. Somewhere along the line, however, I realised that my heart was elsewhere. Over the period of a year, I took time to think of what I wanted to do for the rest of my life that would bring me fulfillment. I researched, met with mentors, went to seminars, read books, prayed, and when I was sure that I had found my calling (and the new direction my life needed to take), I made my exit from banking.

It is okay if you start on a particular career path and then realise along the way that it isn't for you. Remember that the knowledge and skills you've already picked up will be with you forever and will come in useful no matter what you do. Don't try to stick to it simply to prove a point. Instead, assess what you really want to do, what gives you joy, and then go for it. However, there is a thin line between following your passion and becoming a wandering generality. You will see some people who are so fickle; one day they are going for a career in finance, next they are trying to run their own business, and when it doesn't work, they realise that they love to sing and try that too. Remember action with no vision is just passing time. Sticking to a vision is the way up.

A word of caution: Don't stop everything that you are doing to chase your dream. You must apply wisdom and progress carefully. You wouldn't find me advising an individual to drop out of university to pursue a dream; neither will you hear me encouraging someone to quit their job to pursue a dream with no real plan or road map in place. Below are a few real-life examples of people who are going about it the right way and are heading for greatness.

A friend of mine has a vision of owning a big clothing label and a record company. On leaving university, he didn't bow to the pressure of heading straight for his dream with no experience or money. Rather, he joined one of the best banks in the industry and, on the side, continued working towards his vision. Now, people are wearing what was once a dream, and although he is still with the bank, his dream is gradually becoming a reality. When the time is right, he will go with his dream and work on his business full-time.

Another friend, who has a vision of owning a very successful asset management firm, started off in banking and at the same time, started his own firm. He is learning the business from the best and making valuable contacts whilst he has the backing of a big bank, which, incidentally, used to be the same size as his start-up firm.

Another friend wants to run the firm she works for and is keen on becoming a governing voice in her industry. Sit down with this woman and you will quickly sense that she is well on her way. I could go on about various people who have great visions and are going about achieving their dream in a prudent manner, but one final example is a friend who has a vision of owning a big art gallery. Interestingly enough, he is an accountant (a career he is passionate about) and he has set up a company of his own that trades art.

All these people are taking time to learn about their industries and make contacts. Eventually, they will be able to devote all of their resources to chasing their dream full-time. The future that you envision is within your reach.

So, what is your vision: to become the CEO of a corporation or a bank, a partner in an accounting, law or consultancy firm, a politician or a business owner? Great! As the popular saying goes, the journey of a thousand miles begins with one step. Irrespective of the industry, getting an internship is the wisest way to begin.

Chapter 2

The Awesome Four: Finding A Way In – The Internship

Matilda

Matilda had known that she would become a lawyer since she was twelve. She may not have known the intricate details, like the area of law she would practice or what heights she would climb to, but she was certain that she wanted to become a lawyer. In her mind, it was impossible to do anything else, and her plan was simple. "I will keep trying until I get it."

One thing I learnt from Matilda was the idea of what it meant to be completely convinced that you are capable of achieving a goal. Matilda could not conceive any reason why she would not become a successful lawyer. I can still picture her with a puzzled face when I asked, "So what happens if you don't get in?" To this, she replied, "I am not thinking along those lines; why wouldn't any firm want me?" That may come across as arrogant, but it wasn't; she really did try to think of a reason but there was none that she could find, and she banned me from asking any more "what ifs." Matilda's resolve would undoubtedly be tested, and we will see whether she was really as keen as I thought.

Leke

Leke was an opposite of Matilda. I nicknamed him "Jack" because he was a "Jack of all trades, a master of none." He knew something about everything. There was never a time when he was unable to shed some light on the issue at hand. He knew more about economy than the economists who prided themselves on their theories, and he was a whiz in IT and Engineering. When I called him "Jack," he would shout, "There is liberty in knowledge!" One thing was certain, whatever he did – be it banking, consultancy or engineering – success was inevitable. In his cramped, untidy room, we would dream of fast cars, big houses and dinners with the high and mighty.

In our dreams, nobody was too far-fetched to have dinner with; after all, we are all human beings, and some of the giants that we dreamed of meeting, at one point, had nothing. Leke was so clear about the future he wanted, he knew that whichever career he chose would lead to his dreams. All he needed to do was decide where to start. He was studying engineering, was interested in the economy and investing and saw himself helping management with strategy. Every time I would talk about how he needed to focus and why he risked becoming a wandering generality instead of a meaningful specific, he would come back with, "I know focus is necessary and I will do so when I decide." As far as he was concerned, "Where you start doesn't necessarily mean that's where you are going to finish, and besides you only worry about the future when failure is an option."

Steve

Steve's vision and goal to become a doctor was crystal-clear. Unfortunately, he was rejected by every medical school to which he applied, but he had locked his sights on his goal and would not give up. He accepted a place for biochemistry and planned on going to medical school afterwards. However, Steve couldn't help but notice the enthusiasm with which his friends spoke about banking or their aspirations to become investment bankers. Often, he would appear uninterested, but he gave himself away whenever he tried to mimic their enthusiasm and say with excitement what he would be doing in a few years and what he would be earning. His friends explained how an understanding of the banking industry would be useful in any endeavour.

One friend in particular said, "If I don't like it after my internship, I can do something else." This caught Steve's attention.

After further probing, Steve was clear about what his friend was saying. "You work for eight to ten weeks, and at the end, you may or may not get a job. Even if you do, you can simply walk away." At this point, Steve had only one qualm, so he said, "It sounds good, but I am not interested in working for free." Thinking that working for free was the only way that such a deal was possible. "No, Steve," his friend said mockingly, "You'll be earning between £600 and £700 a week." Unable to contain his shock, Steve left thinking that £600 and £700 a week for 10 weeks must be the best summer job there was. Now, banking was in the picture, and he thought, "I already have the common denominator for all careers – the drive, brains and a willingness to work hard."

Fatima

Fatima had absolutely no clue about what she wanted to do. She recalls that during A Levels, all she knew that she wanted was to wear a suit to work and be taken seriously – that was her aspiration. On getting to university, she made one good move, and that was choosing her friends wisely. Realising that she was smart but that she had been sheltered most her life and was not clued up on a lot of things, she thought it wiser to hang out with students who had a fine balance – they had brains, work experience and an idea about what they wanted to become. In doing this, she was still obeying her mum's words, "Whatever you become will depend a lot on those you have around you." By the start of her second year, the buzz had begun about internships.

Everybody (at least that was known to her) was going on about the City, and she couldn't understand what all the fuss was about.

As time progressed, her interest in banking developed as a result of peer pressure. "Everyone's doing it, so I might as well…" she thought. She started to hound the friends who knew even a little about her newly found career.

Her next task was to ask her dad for contact information for anyone he knew in banking. Looking back, she says all she did was seek to learn and then act on the information she had obtained. Knowing her personally, I can confirm that money wasn't a motivation. She simply felt that she shouldn't settle for less when there were such great opportunities. She sounded just like me whenever I reflect on the reason for my big vision; I say to myself, "I have one shot at life, so why not make my mark?" There was a bit of talk about accounting, so she decided to keep an open mind and make her decision when she was offered a choice.

The Internship

I think it is worth stressing how important an internship is. Firstly, internships are the main method by which most industries staff their graduate programmes. Secondly, you can save yourself a lot of headache by discovering earlier on whether the dream job you thought you wanted is really for you. A mentor of mine said, 'there is no point getting to the top of the ladder only to realise it was leaning on the wrong wall.' Which sadly is the case for many. Also, when you have an internship, your chances of getting the right job are higher. I could go on and on, but in summary, with an internship, you are one large step ahead of the pack career-wise.

Applications And Networking

As far as application goes, people fall short by making the same common mistakes repeatedly through spelling errors, failing to answer the questions being asked, giving answers that are too short or too long, not highlighting any distinguishing factors, lacking extracurricular activities, blatantly plagiarising other applications, and the list goes on. One day at the bank, we were all busy with work, and suddenly my MD started laughing loudly. We waited eagerly to hear the joke, but he kept on laughing. Pointing to his computer screen, he kept saying, "I can't believe this!" We scrambled to his desk, and we were all in shock. Some guy had sent him an email, wanting to be considered for a role on the team, but his CV was loaded with grammatical and spelling errors (and by "loaded", I mean more than five). Some of them were just ridiculous. There was no point in reading his cover letter because he clearly wasn't going to get the job. If you ever wondered what happens to your application, due to the long wait, it may have been laughed at and then binned or perhaps HR just deleted it due to mistakes found within the application. It is a shame to lose out simply because you had errors in your application; it ruins your opportunity to put your case forward. Knowing that I often make silly mistakes because my hands move faster than my brain, I read, re-read and then ask somebody else to read anything important that's being sent out. Mistakes can always be made, as you will learn from my experience below.

After leaving banking, I met up with a contact named Stanley regarding a potential opportunity, and he asked me to send him my CV so that he could pass it on to his manager (Anita). I hurried home that evening, sent Stanley my CV, and then the wait began. After about six weeks of waiting anxiously to hear from Anita, I received a call from Stanley asking if everything was okay because Anita had been trying to get a hold of me. I was shocked and said, "That can't be so!" He read out my email from my CV and in panic, I ran to my PC and quickly opened my CV, he was right, I had put down the wrong email address, it ended with ".co.uk" and not ".com". After apologising profusely, I convinced him to ask Anita to kindly forward the email and meeting request. I have no illusions and know that the only reason why Stanley was willing to give me the benefit of the doubt after such a blunder was because we had met and he was impressed with me at the time, therefore, he was willing to overlook my mistake. You, on the other hand, may not get such a chance, so please never be too confident, as to think you won't make errors. Always ask someone else to proofread your work.

One day, I was reviewing applications for an event being hosted by my firm. As is often the case when reviewing applications, I was in need of some coffee to keep me awake, that is, until I opened one student's application –

soon I was wide awake, laughing my head off. I clicked on the application and was about to do my usual scan of grades, awards, activities and work experience related to the industry and leaderships positions, before deciding if the application deserved a more detailed review; but to my surprise, I saw four chunky paragraphs. "That's a rather strange way to write a CV." I thought. As I paused to have a closer look, I burst out laughing and couldn't stop. The student had attached a page from what seemed like an essay and was educating me (or whoever he thought would read it) on some science procedures. What was more interesting was that the document was saved as "CV Banking". I can't even begin to imagine how that would have happened, but in any case, I guess the lesson here is to double- or even triple-check that you're attaching the right document.

Take time to work on your application. I have encountered some applications that sent me to sleep, and I have wondered if the applicants realised that they were writing to human beings and not computer screens! Here is a tip – before you send your application, sit down and ask yourself the following questions:

1. Will this be a soothing breath of fresh air for the person reading it? (bearing in mind that they have to read hundreds or even thousands of applications)

2. Is it attention-grabbing? With so many applications being sent, will your application stand out from the rest of the pool?

3. Will the reader be able to feel your passion and your desire?

4. Can the reader tell why they should invite you for an interview rather than someone else who studied the same course?

Finally, use the career advisory service closest to you as a sounding board. Trust me, they help. During my application days, they were instrumental in improving my applications and helping me prepare for interviews.

The reality is that if you are from a lower-ranking university, your biggest hurdle is the application stage. Big companies use the university you attend to filter through candidates, and although you might be the best candidate for the job, you may never even make it to the interview stage for just that reason. If you fall into this category, I am sure you are thinking, "So, what can I do?"

Firstly, your application must be totally error-free. Secondly, you have to work hard to ensure that your grades are high, so that the HR Department would be willing to give you a chance. You should be aiming to get a first-class from the start or as soon as you read this. The next thing that you should master is networking. Network aggressively. Your chances of being invited for an interview will increase remarkably if you can get someone in the company to recommend you. This applies to every student, but you should make an extra effort to network – it must be a high priority. The average university student depends on networking events, but you want to take it a step further and actively seek out the people who can help.

First, look into your personal network, check with friends and family as to whether they know anyone who can help, and if they don't, encourage them to ask their networks (just because they don't personally know someone who can help doesn't mean a member of their network won't). Maximise relationships with lecturers as they might also have useful contacts. A quality performance in their course will enhance their desire to help you. Your aim is to get a meeting with valuable contacts, and although it isn't an interview, be prepared. They must get a feel of how keen you are. Depending on how the relationship progresses, you can be open and let them know that you would like their help through a recommendation. Also, don't limit networking to your universities – build relationships with students in other universities and make enquiries about networking events happening in their university. If anything, a company representative will see it as you taking the initiative and as proof of how keen you are. The earlier you start building a network, the better.

I went to a networking seminar, and the speaker spent two hours reiterating the same point that in today's work environment, the majority of people get their jobs through networking. His audience comprised of working professionals and entrepreneurs, but his point remains valid for students and graduates. He gave examples of numerous individuals who had lost their jobs and found new roles through networking, simply because employers are more willing to hire someone who comes recommended by a colleague or business associate. I can testify to this fact as well. When I left investment banking and wanted to change careers, it was a friend that introduced me to Stanley. All my friends who knew Stanley sang my praises, and he wanted to meet me. I went in, had a nice chat and made a good first impression. I was called back in for further chats with his boss and colleagues (interviews are really chats, when you think about it), and as I followed the tips that I share below, they were very impressed with me and offered me a job with even better pay and a promotion than my previous position. So, you should network, network and network.

Effective Networking

Someone once said, "You are only as strong as your network," and I have to agree with them. I like the way Obi Ugochukwu, an entrepreneur, puts it when he says, "Any network is a good network when you don't have a network." The first network you must build is with your buddies in university; I know, those clowns, right? I am sure that you can't imagine how the class joker might become useful in the future, but trust me, they will. I remember when I finished university, my dad sent me a 16-page letter advising me on the next phase of my life, and he went on about how important it was to develop a good network with my classmates and maintain contact. Well, I didn't take that advice seriously, and I have paid for it dearly, looking everywhere for those people with whom I desperately needed to make contact. So, take my advice and maintain a good network in your university years, far beyond your close friends.

The next phase of networking is when you attend career evenings organised by your university. This is usually your first contact with professionals in the industry and your first opportunity to find out more about the business. Just so you're clear on how important these meetings are, in my final year, I was invited to interviews with Lehman Brothers and Bank of America because of individuals I had met at career evenings. They recommended me to HR. Be very clear that the company does not send professionals to your university just to tell you about their company and what they do. Oh no, they are also there to spot talented individuals. As such, after the networking event, a select few are invited for further networking in company offices, and some are even invited to dinner. Interestingly, it always happens the same way – one set of students comes for the show, ask a few thoughtless questions and make no impression, while another bunch of students come prepared to make an impression. They ask informed questions and show a keen interest, so the company representatives decide to keep in touch with them. To make an impression, all it takes is to ask a few insightful questions and to show sincere interest as the company representatives explain what they do. It is also important to follow up with questions that show you're listening. Also, show your enthusiasm – smile, smile, smile.

I remember one networking event I attended as a company delegate, and as I chatted away, I couldn't help but notice one student in particular. Andy was quiet but came up with some great questions; and as I spoke, he would agree or disagree, giving reasons for his opinion. At some point, the other 10 students in our circle just stood back and watched as we both discussed the state of the economy. By this point, I realised that this student was one to keep an eye on. Then, to prove the point that I was trying to make – that competition is becoming increasing stiff – I asked each student, out of the blue, to state why they were an ideal candidate for the job (I can be mean like that!). I was trying to give them an opportunity to impress me and sell themselves. As each student took their turn, it was clear who the stars were, and Andy didn't disappoint. He led us through his well-thought-out reasoning about how physics was related to banking and how a banking career will help him combine his two passions. Honestly, I had no clue what he was talking about because I was not a good science student, but he was coherent and that sealed the deal – an invitation for an interview. Afterwards, I asked the students who they would hire, and it was unanimous – everyone agreed that Andy was the most impressive in the group. So, how do you maximise these evenings and other networking events like Andy did?

When you attend an event, don't try to meet everybody. As a student, I used to hop from table to table or group to group, and by the end of the evening, I'd have a pile of business cards but no real relationship with anybody. Sending an email would have been pointless because they wouldn't have remembered me, and if I got a response, it would have been a generic "Nice to meet you too" email. Instead, decide which companies are most important to you and prioritise them; you can approach other companies afterwards. Your aim is to have them remember you from that evening and when you send your follow-up email.

It's not an interview, but if they spot you as a star in the making, they will certainly take note of you. Dress smart. A suit isn't necessary, perhaps trousers, a shirt and a blazer for males and the equivalent of that for females. When you go to their stand, target just two representatives – one senior person and someone from HR. Make sure you do some research about the company beforehand, and if per chance you know the names of the company representatives who will be there, do some research on them as well.

Make your knowledge known, and show that you are very keen. One mistake some students make when they attend networking events is that they focus overly on what the company can do for them. You also want to show that your service will be a valuable asset to the company. Talk about what you have learned about the company, and ask questions accordingly. Have a sense of humour, be professional and serious, but allow room for being human – laughter is good for the soul. Have a concise elevator speech about yourself and your interests ready, and be clear about why you like their company. Questions like, "What one thing would you change about your company?" often causes giggles and may help them remember you. Also, be sure to close when the conversation is at its peak rather than waiting until the conversation starts heading downhill. Don't forget to get their business cards before you leave, and take a minute (by yourself) to note on the back of the card a summary of the person and one detail that would help them remember you, possibly something you said. It is imperative that you email them that evening. Don't leave it till later – do not procrastinate. Let them know it was nice meeting them, make a reference to something in your conversation, say you are keen on their company and give an "original" generic or clichéd reason why you are interested in their company, and say that you would certainly be in touch, when you submit an application. Next, make sure you apply quickly and contact them again to ask them whether it would be okay to mention them in the application as someone you know in the company. You can also reference something they've said about the company in one of your answers when you apply, provided it is relevant.

The importance of preparing before your meeting or networking event is commonly underestimated. Most times, people just show up and hope to get along with other professionals or recruiters as the day progresses, which is a sure-fire way to miss out on maximising the evening. One day, a colleague and I were about to head to a meeting with clients, and a few minutes before we left, he asked if I had my small-talk boosters prepared. I wondered what on earth he was talking about. The look on my face shocked him, so he proceeded to explain. He asked me, "You aren't just going to step into this meeting and hope to get along with the client are you? That's silly; you don't leave such important meetings to chance." Now, before I go to any meeting, I take some time to prepare points that I can discuss and use for small talk. If the conversation is losing ground and heading for an awkward silence, I keep it flowing with another topic. As he was explaining this to me, my MD was walking past and asked what he was talking about. My MD concurred, asking me if I thought he simply went to meetings or networking events without giving any thought to how the conversations might flow. Gradually, it started to dawn on me why they both seemed to get along super well with people when we were out networking and why, during our meetings, they were totally at ease. I often wanted to be around one of them when we were with clients because the conversation would flow more easily. So please prepare, role-play and practice before you head out.

When you start building a good network, maintain the relationships you forge. Avoid contacting people only when you need something from them. You have to give as much as you get. So, keep in close contact through emails, meeting up for coffee, etc. I manage my network by using an Excel spreadsheet. Using different tabs, I prioritise my contacts – tab A is for "very important" (contact monthly); tab B "important" (contact quarterly); and tab C "good-to-know" (contact every six months). I then make a note beside each name, recording what they do and any other useful information. I also note the last time I had been in contact via email or phone, and whether we discussed anything in particular. Initially, this task can seem tedious, but once you get the hang of it and don't procrastinate about updating it, you will be just fine. I endeavour to be in touch with at least two or three contacts each week. This process is vital when you start working full-time because, as mentioned above, you are only as strong as your network.

What else are you doing to show your interests? You need to get involved in initiatives and extracurricular activities that show you are serious about your chosen career. For those in their first year, make sure you get some valuable work experience after your first year. Again, this point applies to everyone, but more so to you if you aren't in a top university that recruiters are keen about. I once read an individual's CV, and although she wasn't in a top university, I was keen on meeting her. She got a first-class average in her first year (no matter the university, this is an impressive achievement), was the president of her university's African Caribbean Society, was an active member of the banking and finance society, had an investment portfolio and had been successful in raising sizeable amounts of money for a charity she was passionate about (amongst other things). From my perspective, she certainly deserved a chance, and that's what you want, enough to make the company think you deserve to be called for an interview. Although the individual in this example focused on finance, the same principles hold true regardless of what industry interests you.

What are the alternatives? I know we all want to get a job with those firms that lead the way in our respective industries. Indeed, the whole purpose of this book is to help you do just that; however, if the university you attended seems like a barrier to entry, then seek alternative routes into your industry of choice as you continue pursuing your dream job. Firstly, do your research and find firms within your industry that are open to applicants from a wider set of universities, as opposed to those that target a "select few". You will be amazed at how many small- to medium-cap companies out there that are not necessarily easier to get into (i.e. they don't necessarily have an easier interview process), but which are open to giving students from a wide range of universities a shot at an interview, provided those students can prove their potential.

Secondly, in addition to looking for a full-time role, search for temporary opportunities in the leading firms in your industry. Essentially, what you want is a foot in the door and the opportunity to prove yourself. You may not be starting where you want, but that's okay – it is all in the finish. As you read on, you will see numerous examples of individuals (including myself) who didn't start where we wanted but eventually got there through hard work. I recall a woman who started off in an investment bank as a temp, and years later, she became the head of the recruiting team for Europe, Middle East and Africa (EMEA). Finally, if you can afford to do it, look for work experience, even if it means working for free for a short period of time. Similar to my point about getting a temporary role if needed, you just want to get your foot in the door and prove yourself.

Chapter 3
Interviews

Now that the boring part of applying for a position is over, let's have some fun. This, my friends, is where the real screening begins and you have the opportunity to show what you're made off. I know you're keen to get a job, but lighten up and don't take things too seriously. I once read a story of a man who was asked to bring several copies of his CV and three references to the interview. An hour before the interview, he gave them a call to ask if the interview could be rescheduled because his references were unable to come with him to the interview. Crazy, isn't it? But at least they could tell he was very keen.

I was both excited and scared when I was going for my first interview – excited because it was my first interview and scared because it was my only interview, yes, my only shot, and I just couldn't mess up.

The first step to a successful interview is accepting the fact that, if you have been invited, you have exactly the same chance as anybody else. Many who head to the interview all suited and booted shouldn't have bothered. By thinking there were going to be many candidates more qualified, they lost a fair fight before they even got there. Rather than that, simply say, "May the best person win." Leave it to the interviewers to determine who is best for the position. If the company did not think you had a chance, they certainly wouldn't have invited you, so don't sell yourself short.

I remember gathering with my classmates in the exam hall, waiting to be let in to write our exams. It always baffled me why students put themselves under pressure by allowing other students to ask, "Do you know this, that or the other?" And they panicked if they didn't have a correct answer. I always thought, "What's the point of that? In the next two minutes, I'll be stepping into the hall, and if I don't know it now, then I don't know it."

When they step out of the exam, they would gather to see who had written what and they'd discuss who was right. What's the point? The exam is done, and there is nothing you can do about it except prepare for the next one. Similarly, what's the point of putting yourself under more pressure when you go to an interview by gathering around those who feel it is their duty to tell you all they know and ask you questions you may not be able to answer. Firstly, who's to say they're right, and secondly, no one knows what yardstick the interviewer would use. When a candidate steps out of the interview room looking bruised and battered, naturally, you may feel scared. But think positively. Think that yours will be better, and it just may be, you never know, otherwise, you'll end up putting yourself under even more pressure, and you don't need that at an interview .

The interviewer tries to assess your competence in certain areas. As you prepare, it's important to have the various interview types explained below in the back of your mind and ensure that you confidently show your competence in these areas. The interviewers are looking for students who are well-presented, well-informed, intelligent i.e. quick to understand and learn, hardworking, enthusiastic and passionate.

Ultimately, they want students who have potential. When you go to the interview, you have to show these qualities. The only way you can convince an interviewer that you are diligent and intelligent is through your answers to their questions. Offer multiple examples to prove you have these qualities. As for your presentation, enthusiasm and passion, you need to show that you're the one they're looking for, so your energy must be contagious, just like Matthew, the visionary first-year student I mentioned earlier.

Interview Types

Interviews vary widely depending on the industry, the position being applied for and the interviewer's personal style. When preparing for interviews, you should try to find out what interview style is likely to be adopted by the company. You can learn this either from students who have been interviewed by the company or sometimes the company lets you know what to expect. I have described the most common interview formats below, and I suggest that you practice until you are comfortable with each format.

Historical Interviews

The emphasis, in historical interviews, is on getting to know you. The interviewer wants to know what makes you unique and why you're the individual that they seek. In such interviews, your CV or application is your roadmap to succeeding in the interview. Questions in these types of interviews will relate to your educational history, your achievements and extracurricular activities, and you may be asked to walk the interviewer through your CV while explaining your understanding of the role at their company. The interview will also aim to assess your strengths and weaknesses. If they ask you to identify your weaknesses, you always want to use an attribute that is generally good, but that can be a weakness. For instance, I could say that I have very high expectations of myself, which sometimes leads me to have unrealistic expectations and put myself under too much pressure.

Incidentally, never say that you have no weaknesses, because no one is perfect and you'll just look like you have no personal insight.

Behavioural Or Competency-Based Interviews

Here, the interviewer tries to gauge your future performance by using your past behaviour. You will be asked to describe particular experiences and competencies. For example, you may be asked to describe a situation where you held a leadership position and demonstrated leadership ability, or where you worked on a team and performed a specific role. The interviewer, in this format, is trying to assess your leadership potential, the type of team member you are, and your analytical and problem-solving skills. In this case, choose your examples carefully and in advance. Through practice, you must become able to confidently articulate your examples and highlight the specific skills that are most important. Many individuals fail to maximise their opportunity with such interviews, which is a shame because this is a good chance to put your best foot forward.

Case Study Interviews

Here, you will most likely be given a situation to analyse, and you will be asked to provide an opinion on how the problems at the core of the situation can be addressed. The focus here is on your problem-solving and creativity ability. So, if asked how many golf balls it would take to fill a room, you can bet that the interviewer wants to assess your thought processes. For example, you could say, "I can't give you a definite answer, but this is how I would go about calculating it, using a few assumptions. I will assume the room is rectangular in shape, and I will first calculate the volume of the room. Then, let's assume we have a small box that can hold 100 golf balls. I would calculate the volume of that small box. Finally, the volume of the room divided by the volume of the box multiplied by 100 will give an estimate of the number of golf balls that would fill this room."

You could use your own creativity. There is really no point, though, in me giving you answers to potential interview questions because we are all very different, and it is of utmost importance that you be yourself. Also, scripted answers are often easy to detect.

Interview Success Criteria

Presentation

A quick word on the criteria you are being assessed against. The rule here is simple – keep to standard business colours. Blue, grey or black suits, and for the women, this could be a skirt or trouser suit. I once interviewed a guy who confidently walked into the room in a black suit (first rule obeyed), but wore a white shirt with a white tie. I felt he hadn't done his homework, but luckily for him, he was too smart, enthusiastic and keen to be rejected. Another guy was wearing a brown suit with a brown shirt and yet another one wore a black shirt. If you are ever confused, you can never go wrong with a white shirt and any colour tie, or just visit the shops and look how the mannequins are dressed. As for women, keep your skirts about knee-length, shirts buttoned up and make sure your attire is neither too tight nor too loose-fitting. Dress so the interviewer focuses on assessing your competence rather than your outfit.

I know, for many, money can be scarce, but that is no excuse. Save up to buy a fairly decent suit or outfit, or beg your folks and family to assist you. I have kept the suit which I used when I was in university to remind me of where I've come from, and when the pressure is on, I wear it and say to myself, "You have come a mighty long way." It looks sad compared to the tailored suits in my current wardrobe, so I know what it's like not to have the money to buy a killer suit, but there are many places to get a decent suit at a good price. So, no excuses – you must look good. A final point: please, please, please do not go into the interview room chewing gum!

Knowledge

For a lot of students, this is their downfall. They simply are not up-to-date on the happenings of the industry or the company. Most times, trying to bluff your way through an interview just doesn't work; it gives the impression that you aren't eager, and interviewers can see right through this. To be honest, it is quite irritating and often gets on the interviewer's nerves as they feel you have wasted an opportunity that someone else could have maximised. Similarly, trying to cram all you can the day before is like playing Russian roulette – either you're lucky or unlucky – it basically leaves your valuable opportunity up to chance. Successful students that excite the interviewers are those who aim to know everything they can about their industry and the specific company as well. To them, reading up doesn't feel like work because they have a vision and they recognise that this preparation is part of the journey. The key here is, as the saying goes: tiny drops make an ocean. When I was looking for an internship, I set aside time each day to read up on the industry. Plan to gain knowledge on your industry every day, just as you do while going to lectures. You will be amazed what reading for 30 minutes a day will do for you, but you must be consistent. Also, don't just read to accumulate standard knowledge, read purposefully to understand, and investigate those issues that you don't understand. It was always apparent which students knew their stuff and which tried to cram the day before. Well-informed students come across as being more confident, diligent, passionate and interested. So again, aim to read for 30 minutes each day; as simple as it may sound, a lot of students don't do this, and they can pay dearly for it.

If I asked you what most sport stars have in common, you'd probably say that at an early age they started playing their game and kept at it until they became superstars. In the same way, you must start early to read up and practice the skills that are required for success in your future career. The habit of daily learning and practice doesn't automatically start once you get a job and start working. No, habits are cultivated over time, and the earlier you start the better. Take a leaf out of Matthew's book, and each day, pay tribute to your goal and career aspirations. Truly successful people are those who identify what they want to become and make each day count. That's why there are only a few who become a governing voice in their industry. One day, I was in a seminar and the speaker asked, "What do you want to be?" People started shouting out their aspirations: "I want to be a top banker…a bestselling author…a renowned athlete…a partner in a law firm…I want to own a consultancy company." After all the shouting, he smiled and said, "I want to be, I want to be, I want to be…but will you be? All of you have stated possibilities, but whether your aspirations come through depends on whether or not you make the daily direct debit to ensure you will become your dream."

In one interview I had, I passionately described how much I wanted to work for a bank, how they were a leader in the industry, and how I wanted to be with the best. It was going very well, and then I was asked which deals they had done recently that caught my attention. Even I was shocked to discover that I had no clue which deals they had been involved in recently. I kicked myself after that interview It had gone well, but that one gap in my knowledge cost me that opportunity.

Intelligence

Some say that you're either intelligent or you aren't. I'd say that's rubbish; you are intelligent and simply need to play according to your strengths. Is the award-winning artist less intelligent than a scientist? No, the scientist is no better in painting than the artist is in manipulating formulas. When I was in structured finance in investment banking, the work on my desk was divided between portfolio management, legal and modelling. I absolutely hated the legal aspect, but did that make me less intelligent than other people on my team? No. My colleague was an ex-lawyer, so she focused on the legal aspect, and I focused on modelling – we each focused on our strength. In reality, the so-called "very intelligent" guys aren't always the most successful. No, it's the guy who is intelligent, hardworking and good with people that makes it to the top, while the "very intelligent" people often end up working for them. Besides, as I have said before, the work you are going to do isn't rocket science; so, provided that you're literate and willing to learn, you're good to go. I remember once, after a long day of interviewing prospective candidates, all the interviewers gathered at the end of the day to discuss which student should go through. One guy had been brilliant in his interview and presentation, but had an average performance on his numeracy test. Some of the interviewers wanted to reject him, but another interviewer got very upset and asked, "For the work we do, are you saying his educational background isn't enough?

Come on, guys." Everyone was humbled, and we put him through. Most times, an application is denied because the candidate was poorly informed, ill-prepared or unenthusiastic.

Diligence

The truth is that it's tough for an interviewer to tell if you are really hardworking. All they can go by is your track record, what you tell them, and how you sell yourself. In my case, I said, "Hard work never killed anyone," and explained how, in addition to my studies, I had to work part-time, served as the vice president of the African Caribbean Society, played football, hosted parties and was in a relationship. I explained how, although it was a tight schedule, it was only possible if I managed my time efficiently, was hardworking and liked working under pressure. That sort of answer, said with a smile, would win an interviewer over. So, take time to think about why you are hardworking and how you can convey that information effectively. Please don't take on too many initiatives just to prove this point though! Studying, extracurricular activities and fun are all necessary in university, so ensure that you have the right balance.

Enthusiasm And Passion

You must show that you're keen, interested and excited to even be there in the interview room. Smile, smile and smile. Be alive when you go to your interview, in spite of how you feel. You should aim to be remembered for your eagerness and your positive attitude. At one of those end-of-day discussions, a student was given a chance not because she was super-intelligent or the most well-informed candidate, but simply because of her enthusiasm. The interviewer said she was the most enthusiastic person she had met and would bring a smile to the team. This contrasts with the fellow who had seemed like a dead man because he sat there lifelessly and spoke as if he hadn't eaten for days. Interestingly, he was very well-informed and intelligent, but enthusiasm is equally as important.

Like I said, the work is not rocket science, and seeing that we spend a majority of our time at work, no one wants to sit next to a 'dead man'. I saw the importance of enthusiasm after my first and only interview of my second year. When I received the much anticipated call, Jason described how much the interviewers had liked me, my energy and passion, but he also said that there was one problem – it was impossible to believe that someone who had gotten an A in A-level math could perform so poorly on the numeracy test. By this time, I thought it was over, but to my surprise, he reiterated that the interviewers really liked my passion. They had actually concluded that my performance on that test must have been due to nerves as it was the first thing I had done. So, I was invited to retake the test. In case you don't know, that's very rare. This proves that enthusiasm is vital to your success and makes it easier for people to make exceptions for you.

Inquisitiveness

At the end of the interview, more often than not, you would be asked if you have any questions, and your answer should categorically be "yes". Having no questions makes you appear unprepared and uninterested. Be careful with your questions, though, you should keep it simple and ensure that you engage the interviewers. People like to talk about themselves, so keep the interviewer interested by asking questions like "What do you like or dislike most about your job and your firm?", "If you had the opportunity, what would you change about this firm?" or "You're living my dream. What's the secret to your success?" Regarding the company, you may also want to ask some questions about their internship programme, its structure, their decision process, tips on how to prepare before starting, etc.

Some students foolishly show their lack of attention and creativity by asking questions that have already been answered during the interview. It is essential to have questions prepared, but be attentive and avoid asking one of your prepared questions if it has already been answered. Another area where students fall short is when they ask boring questions in a bid to seem keen. For example, some students start asking technical questions like "What's your view on the stock market?" Whilst this is generally not a bad question, it has two shortcomings: firstly, it is expected and shows no creativity, and secondly, it can backfire because the interviewer can throw it back at you. Therefore, it is best to play it safe. It isn't wise to say everything you're thinking. Case in point, I once interviewed a guy who asked me the most stupid question you can imagine. He walked into the room, sat down and, while we were waiting for my colleague and having a general chat, he asked me how old I was and then went on to tell me I looked younger, almost implying that I shouldn't be interviewing. As you can imagine, he didn't get the job, with this approach. Therefore, you should keep it simple, keep the interviewer engaged and show your interest.

Be Yourself

Too many people head off to an interview aiming to be what they think the interviewers want. Picture in your mind, one of those films where a goody-two-shoes teenager tries to act like the more popular kids; rather than a preppy shirt and chinos, he switches to an oversized t-shirt, baggy jeans and Timberland boots – all to catch the attention of his beauty queen. What usually happens? He is visibly uncomfortable, looks stupid, trips on his boots and although he catches her attention, she and her friends end up giggling, and that door of opportunity closes forever. More often than not, applicants end up being like that teenager who could have gotten his sweetheart if he had just stuck to being himself. Remember, they don't need two of the same people. My advice is that you are uniquely you, and in doing that, you will not only be successful but also have a good time while succeeding. While we're on this subject, it's important to note that this point is equally relevant during your internship and your career as a whole. The simple truth is that people can never consistently be who they aren't. Eventually, the real you will come out and make you look like a liar and fraud. Save yourself the hassle, and just be good old you. If your employer doesn't like you, then that's fine, you'll get another role more suitable for you. We all have areas we need to change, so be you but be willing to change the parts of you that won't get you far.

If you're wondering what needs to change, take note of what people complain about and ask good friends and family. I find that they are willing to tell you the truth because they want you to make it.

Know Your CV And Application Inside Out

I had already finished writing this book, when I decided to go back and include this point because I thought if I could make a silly mistake like not looking at my CV, then someone else can too. Once, I was preparing for an interview and reading through the company's website, when I saw a video link for interview tips. Naturally, I clicked and started to listen attentively, after all, who can better advise me than the company itself. I was meant to leave home in an hour, and was multitasking heavily, but luckily, I didn't miss the most important part of the video clip that said, "Make sure you can talk through your CV comfortably."

In a panic, I scrambled to my computer. I had been preparing for the types of questions that I thought they would ask, but I hadn't reviewed my CV at all to refresh my memory of what I had included and focused on. If you're thinking, "How could you not know what was on your CV?", then that might be why you have been rejected thus far because you aren't tailoring your CV to the company and the specific role to which you are applying. I quickly read through "Uche's CV company G version," and indeed, I was relieved because I had included several details that I had forgotten about. As you can expect, when I arrived at the company, each person that interviewed me brought out a copy of my CV and focused on a different part. One person actually asked me specific questions to see if I would use the examples I had put on my CV. In conclusion, be sure that you know what's on your CV and application form and that you can talk through those points comfortably.

Firm Handshake

I actually practised my firm handshake with friends numerous times. A firm handshake communicates that you're confident, not intimidated and it gives a good first impression. This point should be self-evident, but a word of caution, keep those sweaty palms dry. If you're nervous and have naturally sweaty palms, then please ensure that your hands are dry, a quick wipe on your trousers or skirt should do the job. Shaking a sweaty hand is unpleasant; plus, it screams out, "Not confident!" On the issue of confidence, I recently asked my friend Femi, why he was so confident when he went for interviews. A day earlier, a few friends had asked him to teach them how to be confident in interviews because his feedback points from interviews consistently mentioned his confidence. He said, "You see, Uche, most times, students go for an interview and forget that the company actually needs them as much they need a job. When I go for an interview, I often say to myself, 'If they didn't want me for the job, they wouldn't be inviting me,' and I'm also very aware that I'm also doing an interview…I'm interviewing them." He added, "As much as I am there to answer their questions, I also go to assess whether the company is right for me. They usually want to tell me how great they are and why the company is a good place to work." I found his comment interesting and asked if he ever got nervous. Femi said, "No, nerves are forever counterproductive. I might want to work for that company badly, but at the end of the day, if I don't get an offer, it's not the end of the world. I prepare thoroughly, so much so that if I don't get the offer, I know I couldn't have prepared more than I did. As is the case with life, something will come up for those that are prepared and persistent. As the saying goes, 'You win some, and you lose some'."

Direct Answers

Answer the question being asked, and not what you think the interviewer wants to hear. In your answer, you can include other plus points, as in the example I gave about demonstrating your diligence, but make sure that it is relevant. Commonly, a student is asked to prove he is a team player, and he starts by discussing his role on the rugby team, but spends most of the time talking about the tenacity required by the sport and then ends with something about how you need to be a team player as well. Whilst tenacity is great, that's not the question that was asked. A smart student explains how they enjoy working on a team as 'no man is an island' and that they find it exciting to build relationships. They give examples of how effective collaboration has been instrumental in their ability to meet some tight deadlines (e.g. projects, organising events), and they conclude that working in a team is fulfilling because it enables them to help others with their weaknesses and vice versa, such that everybody wins. As far as direct answers are concerned, please don't be like the man I read about who, when asked to describe his ideal job, said, "I don't know, I haven't had it yet." Can you imagine that? Be direct, but also give the right answer, which, in this man's case, should have been a detailed description of the role for which he was applying.

Eye Contact

This goes hand-in-hand with a firm handshake. You can't be shaking someone's hand and looking down (this screams out, "Not confident!") or looking over their shoulder, (this suggests that they're unimportant). Also, when you're being interviewed, tame those eyes of yours. With some students, their eyes roam everywhere as though they're hearing different voices and are trying to address each one. The interviewer is right there in front of you, so keep your eyes fixed on him or her. Granted, your eyes will wander off every now and then, but please keep the wandering to a minimum. Like the sweaty palm or shaky handshake, it screams that you are insecure and afraid, which is very different from the natural nerves that everyone has.

"Give Me A Second"

Many students fall short by speaking impulsively without thinking. You cannot prepare for every possible question or guess how a question will be asked. So, you may be asked an unexpected question that throws you off-balance. Do not panic, and certainly don't start chatting away. It's okay to say, "Please give a second to collect my thoughts." Then, do just that, think quickly (i.e. take a few seconds) and deliver a clear answer. Do not waste those seconds by focusing on how clueless you are about the question. No, that's no good and will only make you panic more. You'll be amazed at what your brain will come up with when tasked to think up an answer on the spot.

"I Don't Know"

When we go into interviews, we aim to have an answer for every question; unfortunately, though, some questions may leave you clueless. If this happens, you can begin by asking for a second to collect your thoughts, but then if you really don't know the answer, it's better to admit it rather than trying to wing it. Whilst winging it may work sometimes, more often than not, it rubs interviewers the wrong way and may lead you to get caught out when they ask you to elaborate further. So, play it safe, and a simple "Sorry, I don't know the answer to that question, but I will find it once I leave here," is better. Then, you can do justice to the next question.

Industry-style Questions

Ensure that you're well-versed in the IQ/scenario-type questions that are common in your industry. Most times, there isn't a right or wrong answer; the interviewer is simply trying to assess your thinking process. As long as you have practiced answering a lot of these questions, you will be able to answer questions you've never heard before. I remember when I got through to the second interview at the now-defunct Lehman Brothers; everything was going well until the interviewer asked me how many tyres there were in Germany.

You could literally hear a pin drop. I was clueless, and rather than admit I didn't know the answer, I spewed out a random number. At that point, even I knew it was over. The next blunder happened in the third stage of the same interview process when everything was going well, and then suddenly, I was asked how many people go through Heathrow in a year. I felt like saying to myself, "Don't bother, it's all over." Well, needless to say, I didn't get through to the next stage, and the feedback was as I had expected – great candidate but falls short on problem solving. What was more annoying was telling people this story and having them tell me that those questions were standard. So, why didn't I know this beforehand? I wasn't prepared enough. It would be shameful to lose out because you failed to prepare for obvious questions. Looking on the bright side, though, it was a good thing the interview went badly; otherwise, I would have found out on the news, on that fateful Saturday in September 2008 when Lehman Brothers filed for bankruptcy, that I was losing my new job. I guess some disappointments are blessings in disguise.

Are You Entrepreneurial?

Some students are entrepreneurial by nature; they have no plans of working for anybody and want to start building their dynasty straight out of university. Others, though entrepreneurial, plan to get a job, enhance their skills and eventually start their own business. The point to note here is that, in an interview, you want to be focused completely on your keen interest in the company. It is okay to sell your entrepreneurial nature as an asset to the company; indeed, companies value people who can spot opportunities, gaps or trends and take advantage of them. However, passionately talking about your business plans or an existing business you have already set up will most likely cause the company to doubt your level of commitment and view your plans as a potential distraction from your responsibilities at the firm. Companies want to know that you are committed to them in the long term, so you want to be careful not to come across as wanting to use them as a means to an end.

Body Language

Never forget that communication is only seven percent words. You often see students who come in and tell you how they are so keen for the opportunity, but meanwhile their body language is saying," I don't care, I just want a job." Okay, I know that may be the truth, but at least mask it during the interview! You should see each interview as your only opportunity, and so you should give it your all. No slouching, sit up straight, and lean forward when you want to stress an important point or express your interest.

Don't Give Up

It's not over until it's over. It has happened repeatedly, when an applicant finishes an interview and is confident that he or she has bagged the job, only to receive an email saying "Sorry, but no thanks." On the other hand, an applicant is convinced that the interview couldn't have been worse, and then they get the offer. I remember one interview where I had to give a presentation on how I would advise a company in trouble. After each point, I made, the interviewers would grill me as if the point was weak. The interview grinded onward, and I honestly thought I had lost the opportunity. Nevertheless, I stood my ground and remained positive and engaged. To compound it all, at the end of the interview, one of the interviewers said, "Thank you for your thoughts, but assuming that all of your proposals were wrong and wouldn't work, what would you tell your client? Would you tell them that you couldn't help?"

I was clearly taken aback and asked for a second to collect my thoughts. Miraculously, I came up with an answer. He was visibly impressed by my tenacity and my refusal to back down. I know this because he was one of the interviewers from the assessment centre where Jason had said, "They loved you, but your numeracy was bad." Had I lost hope, it would have been a different story – I would not have been invited back to retake the numeracy test which I passed and as a result I got my only internship offer.

Breaking The Rules

On one particular assessment day, I broke most of these rules; and needless to say, I didn't get the job. In my final year, I had my first-round interview with Bank of America and felt on top of the world. The interview couldn't have been better; I had answered the questions well and was full of energy.

Sure enough, I was invited for the final round, but then I dropped the ball. Why? Because I had become overly confident. I hadn't prepared sufficiently, and I had become complacent. I stepped into Bank of America looking sharp in a black suit, blue shirt, red tie and well-polished shoes, so I got an A on the well-presented part. I walked into the interview room, did my well-practiced firm handshake, and sat down to have a nice chat with my two interviewers. It was going well initially, and then I made my first mistake. He asked why I wanted to do investment banking (I'm sure you're thinking, "How can he mess that up?"). In response, I spilled out my usual answer, but then I added, "Plus, I like investing."

The smile on his face told me I should have stuck to my usual blurb. Then, he asked what my top three investments would be. At this point, I should have asked for a second, knowing that whatever I said would be followed by "Why?" but, stupidly, I listed the first three that came to mind – property in Nigeria, stocks in the UK and paintings. I should have mentioned only that which I could comfortably and confidently discuss. Clearly, my body language was saying that I was uncomfortable and didn't know the answer, but my mouth started moving faster than my brain, and I said, "Diversification is good, and they are all good investments." I had nothing to support my reasons for wanting to invest in these assets. This showed that I hadn't done my research, and I came across as uninformed.

By this time, I was sinking into a posture that displayed my anxiety and fear. He looked like he was losing his patience and glanced around the room. I thought he might want to throw something at me for wasting his time and then, pointing to the painting behind him, he asked how much the painting had cost. "How was I supposed to know that?" I thought. What came next was almost the last straw, I asked him which painting. Now, there were only two paintings, and he had clearly pointed at one, so my response couldn't have been worse. I was stalling. Patiently, he pointed to the painting again and waited to hear the next genius answer I would come up with. In hindsight, I had two options – I could have admitted that I didn't know or I could have asked for a second. Perhaps if I asked for a second, I would have remembered renowned artists and said, "It depends on who painted it. Is it a Picasso or a Da Vinci?" but rather without thinking, I gave some random number. He was completely shocked. He laughed out loud and simply said, "Thank you for coming."

Next up was the numeracy test. I was ready for this, or so I thought. When they handed out the test papers, I couldn't believe it – it was the same exact test that Jason said I had performed so poorly on, but I hadn't prepared enough for it, and I started to get nervous. I wasn't surprised when the HR lady came around later and told me I had gotten the answers to the practice questions wrong again. I knew even before I opened her email a few days later, that I wouldn't get the offer. Truthfully, I didn't deserve it. I hadn't done my homework. So, take heed and make sure you don't blow up golden opportunities like I did with that one.

Internet

In the current world, you should be very careful about what your online profile looks like. It is simple, if I Googled your name, what would come up? I am sure you have heard the stories of people who lost their jobs or great opportunities because of indecent pictures or entries on the Internet. I personally believe that, as time progresses, our online profile will be just as important as our traditional CVs. My advice is always to play it safe, do a Google search on your name and make sure there isn't anything on there that could cost you golden opportunities. Likewise, what interesting facts do you want me to find out about you if I Googled your name? You may ask me whether there is a high chance that a recruiter will read your CV and then search for you on online? Answering that question is like trying to guess the identity of the recruiter that will review your application – you just never know, so it is best to play it safe and assume that they will.

Product Mentality: Your Way In

You will succeed if you clue in to the fact that, when it comes to recruiting, students are products and the company is the buyer. With this in mind, put yourself in the company's position and assume you were trying to buy a car without any financial constraints. Would you go for a Benz CLS or a Fiat Punto? Pretty easy decision, right? In the same way, some students are clearly like a Benz – they have dedicated time and effort to preparing themselves, while others are Puntos, whose only real qualification is that they managed to get into university. Now, if you agree that you won't see rich people strolling into a Fiat showroom to check out a Punto or any other Fiats, then why are you, as a Punto, hopeful that the Goldmans, McKinsey, Clifford Chances or KPMGs of the world will be interested in you? With this analogy, you can easily see why some students don't make it; they are simply no match for the other products on offer and no buyer is going to pay £35,000 for a Punto. Employers want the best, and if you have spent time preparing to such an extent that your interest, dedication and capabilities are obvious, then you won't be in the showroom for long.

You need to ask yourself honestly which category you fall into and then strive to do better. It is best to recognise that you are a Punto and then diligently apply yourself to become a Benz, rather than have the false perception that you are a Benz, when you really have a long way to go. When you interview, you are both the product and the salesman trying to convince the buyer to buy. Therefore, go along each day thinking, "Am I becoming a Benz?" Remaining a Punto or, even worse, going from being a Benz to being a Punto should not even be an option.

No Place For The Undisciplined

After all is said and done, the reason why most students fall short is lack of preparation. This issue of preparation relates not only to your career but to your degree as well. If you're serious about success and believe you will succeed, then you don't start preparing only when the opportunity presents itself. No, you start long before the opportunity arrives, and it is your preparation plus the opportunity that will lead to your success. Spend 30 minutes to an hour each day to read and practice. Your industry of interest determines what you read. Websites are always a good place to start and interestingly, once you start, more suggestions should pop up.

Do mock interviews with friends, visit the career advisory service, and speak to other students who have already been successful at interviews. The key here is consistency, and over time, you will become confident, well-informed, competent and every company's dream. Time is the greatest test; a lot of students start with a bag of energy and, in no time, fizzle out. This inconsistency is the reason why some students are unsuccessful. I can never forget my final exam in my first year. I was drifting in and out of sleep and twitching like a drug addict. Thinking about it, I was addicted to the artificial energy of Red Bull because I had been largely partying and going out with friends instead of studying, and I would have failed woefully if I hadn't pulled consecutive all-nighters.

As I was an international student paying close to £10,000 a year, failing was simply not an option. Till this day, I don't know how I passed that exam! I'm not saying that you shouldn't have fun, but make sure that while you're having fun, your studies aren't suffering. Remember that there's a time for everything. A time to study, a time to prepare, and a time to play – just make sure that you balance things and don't leave preparation until the last minute. Always remember that we are forever deciding between two options – either we "play now and pay later" or "pay now and play later." Often, we tend towards the first option but eventually regret it and wish we could rewind time. I implore you to have a great time in university, because I know I did, but when it comes to your career, decide to pay now by learning, little by little, on a daily basis, and then you will enjoy the playing even more.

Be warned, procrastination is waiting at the door. We've all been there. We decide, with utmost conviction, that we are going to stick to a new routine, and then before long, your commitment has become a thing of the past. We gradually put off what we planned today to do tomorrow, and after a while we don't even bother anymore. After all, there is no interview in sight anyway. Remember that all the preparation you are doing isn't just for an interview, it's for your internship and, ultimately, your career. If you're going to be successful, you must be disciplined. The bridge that connects a thought or a dream to its manifestation is discipline. Apart from a lack of discipline, the other excuse for procrastination is being too busy. If you can't set aside time to prepare, then you are too busy and need to drop something. Don't procrastinate, make a personal commitment and discipline yourself. Please don't be like the many that want the prize, but are unwilling to pay the price.

Finally, on the issue of preparation, don't be deceived. You don't know what other students are doing in their closets, particularly those who appear to be playful and who seem like they won't get far. You may be surprised to learn that those students who you think are messing about may actually apply themselves diligently in private and end up being the successful ones. On my graduation day, most of us were in shock when the dean announced the only student who finished with a first. This guy was a party animal, but was clearly doing something right when alone. Run your own race, follow your plan, and don't compare yourself to others.

One day, my dad called me, and, in an effort to explain why I should not compare myself with anyone else, he told me the story of Obi Nwokoloko, a friend of his from his university days. Obi was a Math student, and he was generally considered to be going nowhere fast. His daily pattern was something like this: during the day, he would miss lectures, and by early evening, he would be in the girl's hostel flirting around. Later on, like most students, he would end up in the bar having a few drinks and a laugh. No one ever took note that Obi left the bar early and, if they did, they assumed he was going back to the girl's hostel to hang out. When students saw him with lecturers, they did not think much of that either.

What students did not know was that Obi was a very smart individual and he worked best at night. Over time, students would make fun of him and gleefully warn him that if he didn't change, he'd end up a bum. In those days, final-year university results were posted on the wall in the department, perhaps to motivate students to perform well. On that fateful day, there were some students that smiled and some that cried, and then there was one student who did not do as well as he had expected. To console himself, he looked below to see what Obi got. "At least I will do better than Obi," he thought. The lower he looked, the happier he became thinking Obi had really flunked. Getting to the end, he turned to a friend," I think Obi has been dismissed, I can't find his name." His friend, to continue the joke, said, "Maybe he came first in the class," and proceeded to look up towards the top of the list. To their surprise, Obi had indeed come first and had even received an award.

Next time you are out with friends, having a good time and thinking it is okay not to study and prepare because you are all out and about, remember Obi Nwokoloko.

Chapter 4
The Awesome Four:
Optimistic Outlook

Matilda

Matilda was cool, calm and collected when everybody was making noise about internships. In her case, she was very well clued up, because her older brother had done his rounds and was already working in the City. In light of her background, she felt it would be a walk in the park. She used to ask herself questions like "Why won't I get a place? Don't they want the best?" Some might call her proud, but I call it confidence and a good estimation of one's worth. In addition, I know her, and she was one of those whose confidence can easily be mistaken for arrogance. She thought she could apply to her top five, get offers and choose, but little did she know that her confidence would be tested.

One day, when I looked at my phone after Macroeconomics and saw ten missed calls from Matilda, I started to panic. When I finally spoke to her, she said, "Uche, I can't believe it, I'm 20 applications deep, and I still haven't been invited for an interview. I attend a top university, have good grades, yet still have no interview invite! I don't know what the problem is." I could definitely appreciate where she was coming from. I was also still waiting to get an interview after submitting many applications. I asked her what she was going to do. "Are you going to give up and try again next year?" She laughed for a bit and said, "Give up? Give up? You must be joking! Once this paper is over, I would speak to a few people who have been called for interviews and get application tips. I'll get them to read over my application, and I will continue to apply until I get an interview." "But what if nothing comes up?" I asked. She said, "Well I haven't considered that yet, and I won't need to.

All I know is that I will get an offer and if, for reasons beyond my control, I don't, I will cross that river when I get there. Besides, there are a number of small solicitor firms that would love assistance during the summer, even if I have to do it for free; one thing is for sure, I am not going to be a waitress this summer."

After she hung up, even I was re-energised. I quickly erased the thought that had started to build regarding what I would do if no offer came through – such thoughts were banished from that day.

Fatima

Fatima had an experience similar to Matilda's. Fatima had only just clued up in second year, so, for her, anything would have been better than doing nothing and asking daddy for some pocket money. She didn't seem as bothered as my other friends, who became distraught each time they received a rejection letter from big banks, law firms or consultancies. One day, while I was chatting to her, she told me she had just spent some time consoling a friend who had just received yet another rejection letter. "What's the big fuss?" she said. To which I replied, "You don't care, that's why you aren't as bothered." She didn't find that funny, and she screamed into the phone, "You call 30 applications 'not caring'? You know what? Get off my phone!" I had to repent that day, firstly, because I had no clue she had sent in 30 applications, and secondly, because I had misinterpreted her great attitude as not caring. She told me, "I applied to the big banks like everybody else, but I also applied to a lot of smaller houses. In fact, I applied to them first to see if my application was any good. As it stands, there are still a few big banks I haven't applied to, and I plan to do so as soon as I get whatever feedback I can from the places that rejected me. I thought that's the benefit of starting to apply early and having a plan." I told her it sounded like a great plan and apologised for my oversight.

Fatima did not see this as the end of the world, but rather she believed that she would make it. She said, "It seems like all my friends are waiting for a company to tell them they're capable by inviting them for an interview. That's not me; I am not waiting for anybody to approve of me. I tell myself I am good and able, and I see a rejection as the company's loss." She also had a plan in place to meet up with the son of her dad's friend, who worked for Barclays Bank and had promised to look at her application. "He's going to tell me what I've done wrong so that I can work on my application for the remaining banks."

Steve

Steve, following his discovery about the benefit and structure of an internship, went on a rampage. He wanted to know everything about investment banking. Being a complete beginner, his first stop was the career advisory service. After a long chat with an adviser about his discovery, and whether it was worth switching from his initial plan of becoming a doctor, he decided that no knowledge is lost knowledge and picked up a copy of Vault Career Guide to Investment Banking. The words of the adviser kept ringing in his ears, "Look at it this way, if you do it and don't like it, you still win. You get paid a lot of money, and you know one thing you don't want to do, which is as good as finding gold. Plus, you don't want to live in regret and keep wondering in the years to come, 'Should I have…?'"

After going through the Vault Career Guide a few times, he found other useful sources of information, like E-Financial Careers, and went through that website multiple times. Talk about making each day count, Steve wanted to know everything he could. He read so incessantly that one of his friends said, "Mate, are you trying to buy a bank or something? It is just an internship, you know." Steve explained, "Initially, I said to myself, 'I will set out to learn all I can, but if I get bored and it becomes a pain, I know this isn't really for me.' But the more I read, the more I want to know." Steve went on and got himself a place in Capital Chances, who organised a two-day programme on learning about the industry.

His thirst for knowledge became known among his fellow Nigerians in the City. I had been in the industry for two years when I heard from friends that there was a guy who was reading like he was going to sit for an exam. When I finally met Steve and asked why he was reading so much, he said he wanted to be sure he was passionate enough to get into the industry. He believed in applying himself fully to whatever he did. His first five applications were rejected, despite the experience he had gained through Capital Chances. Steve decided to take a step back and figure out why. His next step was back to the careers office, and he started trying to contact ex-students who were in banking, for assistance.

Leke

Meanwhile, Leke was busy having a good time and not putting himself under much pressure. I actually had to start adopting his ways with each rejection I received. I would ask him, "Don't you care?"

Smiling, he would respond, "Uche, the picture of the future doesn't change if I don't get an internship." Leke was always optimistic; he wasn't swayed by the rejections. Instead, he remained upbeat about the big picture. I started to see sense that his was a winning attitude. At that time, Leke had received four rejection letters but was so focused on his brighter future that he didn't let temporary losses keep him down. Unlike Steve, who had to start reading from scratch, Leke had maintained his Jack-of-all-trade status and kept topping up his already vast knowledge base.

The Offer – Don't Stop Until You Get It

Life has an interesting way of testing us to see how badly we want our dreams to come true. Tests come in all shapes and sizes. Your test could be the struggle of getting through to the interview stage or it might be the difficulty of getting a job, but sooner or later, your desire will be tested. The good news, though, is that it is only a test, and as such, it is temporary. Trials can make or break you, but nothing can stop you unless you allow it to.

When you think of successful businesses today and how they started, you will understand why persistence is necessary.

Take the story of the famous chain Kentucky Fried Chicken (KFC). What many people do not know is that, if not for the old Colonel's persistence, we wouldn't be enjoying that delicious chicken today. When he was 66, the Colonel lost his business and started living on unemployment benefits, and that just was not enough. At that age, one would have expected him to have given up, but instead, he made his way through the country trying to sell his fried chicken recipe. He was turned down not 100 times, not 500 times, but 1,009 times before somebody said yes. Of course, the rest is history – he went on to become a multimillionaire at an age when most people retire. So, when your resolve is being tested, simply do what the Colonel did – just keep at it. As I have said and will continue to say throughout this book, only you can stop you. In fact, do something crazy and shout right now, "Only I can stop myself." I keep emphasising this point because if you can accept it, believe it and act on it, then there will be no height you cannot climb.

I remember how it felt to get my first interview after waiting for so long – it felt like a miracle. I did the best I could, and I waited patiently to hear my fate. Waiting can be quite nerve-racking. There I was, walking home after a long day of lectures and literally wondering, "What on earth am I going to do this summer?" Suddenly, my phone started ringing, and when I answered, a woman confirmed that I had been offered a summer internship. Can you believe it? After applying to every investment bank there was, and a number of consulting firms, I had finally been offered an internship.

Once she hung up the phone, I literally fell to my knees; right there on the road, looked up to the heavens and thanked God. Believe me, there isn't a better feeling when you are in university and you get an offer, particularly when it is the one you want or, in my case, your only one! Until then, I had placed a lot of emphasis on preparing to get an offer; however, preparation without the right thinking is a pointless exercise. While in university, I unconsciously cultivated a key ingredient for success – my thinking. I saw no reason why I could not get an internship. For me, it was just a matter of time. Rightly or wrongly, I looked at some people whose performance was less than stellar and thought, "If they could get an internship, why can't I?" I was under no illusion that I was the best candidate for each criterion, but I focused on my strengths and decided that whatever weak areas I had could be strengthened with work. I have come to realise that your thinking plays a fundamental role in determining whether you are going to be successful. Before I even started applying, I was already visualising my first day on the job – I could see my pay cheque, and I had dinner with an imaginary team on numerous occasions. Any chance I got, I spoke to people who had already achieved my dream and, using their description, I formed a better picture. Before I knew it, I was completely convinced that I would make it, and I did nothing but aim to make that picture a reality. Like I said, little did I know that I was already obeying the first law of success. Had I been conscious of this fact back in university, I would have maximised it even more.

STOP! Read t-h-e n--e--x--t l--i--n--e s---l---o---w---l---y: *"Where I will be in the next one year, five years or ten years would be the product of my thoughts and corresponding actions."*

Change Your Thinking, Change Your Life

On the way to success, one fundamental truth is that you gravitate towards your most dominant thoughts. If you won't take it from me, then listen to King Solomon, who said, "As a man thinks in his heart, so is he," meaning that where you are now is a result of your thoughts (and I might add, actions) of yesterday, and where you will be tomorrow results from what you are thinking now. If, from this book, you get nothing else but this point, then your life will be forever changed. This truth will work for you regardless of your previous failures, regardless of whether you attended a top-performing university, and regardless of whether those in your family haven't achieved much. Your mind is the only thing over which you have complete control, and you have the power to control your mind to whatever ends you desire, be it becoming a CEO, a partner or even a business tycoon. The only problem is that most people choose to think negatively and accept that they cannot really amount to much. You are literally what you think, and the quality of your life cannot be better than the quality of your thoughts. In fact, take some time now to think of where you are, and consider what your thoughts have been prior to your current position. The job you get cannot be better than the job you think you are able to get or that which you think you deserve. Your circumstances are only a reflection of who you are inside (i.e. your thinking), and as you change your thinking, you will change your circumstances and, in turn, your life. You must realise that a successful person is successful internally before it becomes externally evident. As such, you must first become a successful intern or graduate in your thoughts, before you actually live it.

It is like taking a picture of yourself wearing a blue shirt, and when you get it printed, you don't like what you see, so you ask the photographer to print the same photo but make the shirt look black without employing the use of technologies like Photoshop. With all the belief and determination in the world, this is impossible. You can spend your life trying to make it possible, but it won't change the picture. You must put on a new shirt and go take a new picture. The mind works in the same way; it prints out in real life all the dreams and pictures we have impressed on it over time.

So, as with the scenario, we must succeed in our internal state of mind before our life will begin to reflect that change. But a lot of students are trying to break this law, trying to be externally when they have not changed within themselves, which simply ends up in frustration. Many students are gunning for jobs in the City and on Wall Street, but their self-portrait does not match their aspirations. Like I said, such students only end up as frustrated quitters. While there are tips geared towards getting ahead in your career, the real work occurs between your ears.

It is important to first realise where you are i.e. whether you think negatively or positively, whether you have a good self-image, and whether you have mediocre or lofty aspirations, and why. Only then, can you change your thinking. If you want to climb out of a hole, the very first thing you must do is to stop digging. Often times, you can dig yourself into a mental hole by thinking negative thoughts. Then, you make it worse by gathering around with other negative-thinking people and you all sink even more rapidly.

If you think it will be difficult, then it will be difficult. If you think that you are an average student, then you will be an average student. If you think getting that job will be impossible, it will be impossible. Stop thinking negatively! "If you want to think positively and productively, the very first thing you must do is stop thinking negatively and destructively," says Jide Iyaniwura, a successful business consultant and investor. Guard your mind! Zig Ziglar says, "You are where you are and what you are because of what's gone into your mind, you can change what and where you are by changing what goes into your mind." In other words, what goes into your mind would determine your position and ultimate identity. You must watch what you read and who you listen to, and you must clear your mind of unrealistic, mediocre and negative words.

At any given moment, you're either feeding your mind negatively or positively, and whichever side you feed more wins the battle. I heard a story of an Eskimo who had two dogs, one white and the other black. He had trained both dogs and used them in dog-fighting competitions. Each week, he went down to the ring, and when the dogs would fight each other, they'd win in turns; if the white dog won this week, the black dog would win the next. Over time, the dogs became old, and the Eskimo had to retire these dogs that had made him so much money. One day, while he was in town, a curious shopkeeper asked him why the white dog would win one week and then the black dog the next, and how come he always knew which dog to bet on. The Eskimo smiled back and said, "I would bet on whichever dog I had fed more that week." If you're going to get ahead, you must feed your mind right. I do this by reading my Bible, inspirational stories, books on success and listening to motivational speakers. What are you reading, and what have you been feeding your mind?

Remember that when your mind expands by focusing on that which is possible, it cannot contract. When I read or hear stories about how people have overcome substantial obstacles to achieve their goals, I am inspired to persevere. For instance, when I read that David Cameron, past British Prime Minister, was director of Corporate Affairs at Carlton Communications at the age of 28, I saw a new target, and my mind accepted the fact that, at 28, an individual can be a Director. The problem with most people, and the reason why they remain followers for their entire lifetime, is that they only focus on celebrating the fruits of success that they see in certain individuals i.e. the nice clothes, classy cars, big houses, etc; they never bother to seek out the qualities that have made these people so successful. I want to know how they have become successful, and you should too and "the how" can be found by reading their books, hearing their stories and listening to renowned speakers who often highlight such successful individuals as examples.

For example, in his book *The Outliers*, Malcolm Gladwell shares results from years of research on individuals like Bill Gates, whose success is not the norm, and he made an interesting discovery that each of these outliers had spent over ten thousand hours working on their skills in their specific industry or business. Now, I may not spend ten thousand hours in study and practice, but at least I now know what it takes to even be half as successful as one these outliers. If you don't already know, an 'outlier' is an extreme deviation from the mean. Malcolm calls these individuals outliers because their success is beyond that which most individuals achieve in a lifetime. Furthermore, reading and listening to interesting speakers is far better than listening to the negative news that is constantly being broadcasted by media channels, like the majority of the population.

As the popular saying goes, you can take a man out of the bush, but you can't take the bush out of the man. Similarly, in the movie Elf, Will Ferrell, having grown up with the elves, was transported back to human society to meet his father. Being around human beings made no difference, as long as he thought he was an elf, he behaved and acted accordingly. Many students are like that, they get a chance at a job, and rather than being influenced by the success around them and letting it influence their thinking and their life, they maintain the same mediocre and negative mindset. That's why, while you see one person go from being a clerk to the Global Head of a division in 15 years, another becomes a Senior Clerk within the same timeframe. I would have been one of the statistics if I hadn't woken up. I thought I could get an internship, but deep down I doubted that becoming a CEO was even possible for me. Even though I said I would be one, I didn't believe it, and even the job offer began to seem unlikely when I saw the calibre of the other interns. But being around successful people during my internship changed my mind, and I became increasingly willing to expand my dreams and my aspirations.

As we discussed before, you must become a successful applicant, intern, analyst/trainee in your thinking first before it can become a reality. Forget what may have happened in the past, and remember that you cannot become more than what you believe. So, think of the past as lessons to learn from (both good and bad) and mistakes to avoid in the future, rather than viewing it as a hint of what is to come. Look to the future with a new eye. Believe that you are successful. Clear your mind of that defeatist mentality, and enjoy the success that awaits you.

There is an interesting story about the National Convention of Barbers and Hairstylists of the United States in Sam Adeyemi's book, *Think and Succeed*, which serves as a good illustration on how impossible it is to become externally that which you have not become internally. The barbers and hairstylists wanted to give their profession a better image, so they hired a PR executive. The first thing he did was to go down to the slums of New York to find a man who was homeless and unkempt. The PR executive's proposal sounded good to the homeless man, particularly because there was money involved, so he went along with the plan. First stop was the photographer's shop to take pictures in his current state. Then, following a steam bath, a shave and a haircut, he went back for more pictures. To top it all off, he took the homeless man to the tailors for some tailored suits, shirts, ties and shoes and then a final round of pictures. On the day of the convention, the executive stationed three life-sized portraits of his subject in the hotel lobby and wrote, "See what the Barbers and Hairstylists of America can do to a man." Naturally, the story hit the headlines, and the convention was a big success. The Hotel Manager was touched by the story and decided to help, so he offered the homeless man a job, which he accepted; however, the homeless man never showed up to work. What went wrong? The homeless man was changed externally, but inwardly, he was the same old defeatist and had gone back to his old lifestyle in the slums. Again, as a man thinks in his heart, so is he. You cannot rise beyond your thoughts.

Over the years, right from the time of King Solomon to the present day, those who have studied the secrets to success have all come to the same conclusion. Take time to ponder these quotes:

"We become what we think." - *Earl Nightingale.* Earl was a renowned American motivational speaker and author. He was also nicknamed "the dean of personal development" and his book, 'The Strangest Secrets' is one of the bestselling motivational books of all times.

"Whether you think you can or you can't, you are right." - *Henry Ford,* founder of the Ford Motor Company.

"The mind is the master weaver, both of the inner garment of character and the outer garment of circumstances." - *James Allen.* James was an author and is known as a pioneer of the self-help movement. He authored a number of bestselling inspirational books and his most renowned work is 'As a Man Thinketh'.

"We can always trace the roots of our circumstances and behaviour to the thought: that dominate our minds. It is only by taking control of our mind that we take contro. of our lives." - Sam Adeyemi. Sam is an author, speaker, and president of Success Power International.

"When we appreciate inside, our lives appreciate outside." - Sam Adeyemi.

As I pondered on quotes like these, I began to say to people, "It is impossible for me to fail, success is simply inevitable." Now, I am not foolish enough to assume that I would not encounter setbacks. I know that I will bounce back each time as I have done in the past, knowing that with discipline, a positive mental attitude, hard work and the willingness to keep pushing, I will achieve my goals".

Take Action

So, I ask you, "What are you thinking?" An equally important question is "What are you doing?" This second part is crucial because action is required to bring your thoughts into reality and it serves as proof that you really believe you can achieve your dreams.

When it comes to the job market, think positively. Start thinking of the job you want. What will the interview be like? What will you wear? What will you say? How will you compose yourself? What sets you apart from the pack? We all have a unique story, but what really makes you different? Dream about your first day on the job and what they will say about you. Experience in your mind's eye what receiving an offer will be like, feel the joy in your heart, and imagine telling your friends and celebrating. Let these thoughts continue day and night, but don't stop with the thoughts, start taking the right steps, start reading up on your industry of choice, and speak to people in that industry and those in your university who have done internships. How did they do it? What's the difference that makes the difference? This is important because the simple truth is that only the best are wanted. Now, if, as you read that last sentence, you thought, "So, that excludes me," then you know you have a lot of work to do. If not, then you know you're on the right track. Just make sure it continues.

Warning: It Isn't Easy To Change Your Thinking

A word of caution: when you start trying to change your thinking, it will be tough at first and you may want to quit. It is always easier to go back to what you are used to, but look at it this way – the average university student is 19-years-old, so your mindset, at the time of graduation, has been developing over the last 19 years. That is potentially 19 years of thinking you are average and aspiring for no more than a job after university or thinking that your future will simply depend on wherever life takes you. It would be foolhardy to believe that you can change your thinking in a week. In fact, it is an ongoing process, but I must say a very fulfilling and rewarding process that will lead to more success than you thought possible. In explaining why change was difficult for a lot of people, Bob Harrison, who teaches strategies for success, said, "Change will never happen until the dream and the desire to change is greater than the pain of change." The first step to changing your mind is to fuel your dreams and desires to such an extent that the discomfort of disciplining yourself is dwarfed by the rewards of the dreams that you envision.

Fuel your dreams by constantly thinking about them, talking about them, and seeing yourself living them. Whatever you do, make sure your dream is big enough and worth the trouble.

I am a good example of how hard it is to change your thinking. Growing up, I always believed that I wasn't as smart as my older brother, and that I had to work and study twice as hard to get grades as good as his. I was completely convinced that if he had to study one hour to understand a subject, I had to study for two to three hours to achieve the same level of understanding. In hindsight, I realise that wasn't true, but as long as I believed it, it was. My thinking became a greater problem when my mind started to tell me that various other people were like my older brother. One good thing, though, was that this false thinking made me study more, but whenever I felt like I had not done twice as much reading as those who were like my older brother (i.e. a lot of my peers), I would expect to perform poorly, and as you know, life has a way of giving you what you expect.

As I shared my self-image with a mentor, he took it upon himself to ensure that the lie I had told myself was erased from my mind. After giving numerous examples of why I was just as smart and how I had the same capability, I thought this defeatist thinking was over. I found myself bringing up the same issue over and over again. Thankfully he was patient enough to keep disagreeing and reminding me of the truth. He set me an assignment to remind myself daily of his words and said, in the first person, "I am just as smart for 1, 2, 3 reasons, and I am just as capable for 1, 2, 3, reasons." As I did that for a while, I gradually started to believe what I said, and my expectations changed. With these changed expectations came better results, but not overnight. Neither did I think it would work at first.

As you know, we all want to consider ourselves successful, so I bought the idea and started to like the new me that I was selling to myself. Interestingly, I have come to see that I am not alone; these things are rarely said in the open because people want to save face, but the reality is that a lot of people have insecurities and similar misconceptions, often nicely masked. Most likely, you will question how true it is that your thinking really influences your life. Then, if you try to renovate your mind, there will be times when you will think, "This isn't working." My advice is not to try to figure it out, but just believe and take a plunge. After all, in the least, we can agree that a positive mindset and a dream of a bright future is far better than a general mood of negativity and being saddened by the uncertainty of what the future may hold. So many successful people have been kind enough to share this secret about the power of the mind, they can't be wrong.

Watch What You Say

In addition to thinking and acting right, take care to speak right as well. A lot students and graduates go on and on about how tough it is to get recruited and then they find it difficult to get recruited. They are reaping the fruits of the seeds they sowed with their words. I didn't realise how important my words were until I read something that King Solomon wrote. He said, "From the fruits of his lips, a man is filled with good things, as surely as the work of his hands." When I read that, I was shocked; he placed the same emphasis on speech as he did on action. The more I thought about it, I realised it was true. It is said that "from the abundance of the heart, the mouth speaks", and if you synthesise that with the idea that "as a man thinks in his heart so is he", then you can deduce that your speech is only a reflection of what exists in your heart and your thinking. It all goes hand in hand – what you believe influences your thinking, and your mouth gladly announces what's going on inside.

Even if you want to become a success, you won't as long as your mouth disagrees with your aspirations. James, in the Bible, puts it best when he said, "A bit in the mouth of a horse controls the whole horse. A small rudder on a huge ship in the hands of a skilled captain sets a course in the face of the strongest winds. A word out of your mouth may seem of no account, but it can accomplish nearly anything or destroy it!' A ship either heads for the rocks or home sweet home, depending on how the captain turns the rudder; likewise, your life heads for a brighter future or a darker one, depending on what you say from the abundance of your heart.

Do yourself a favour and do an assessment of the words you speak. Consciously monitor the things you say over the next week, and you may be shocked to hear how negative you are. I did this recently and found out that I often said "It isn't easy." Now, while that's better than saying "It's impossible", it showed why I usually felt like obstacles were tough and that there was so much work to do. As a result, when I found myself saying, "It isn't easy," I would refuse the statement and shout, "It is easy," and, "I am able!" To further stress the importance of this assessment, note that your mouth is the prophet of your future. Where you will be in a few years isn't hard to discover because, daily, you are prophesying. If I were you, I would get to work and start changing the things you say that are not in line with what you want to become. And if your speech is already generally in line with your aspirations, then make sure to do so more often.

By now, you know how important it is to think success if you are going to be successful, but old habits like negative talk are difficult to curb even when you start getting your thinking sorted out. So, don't stop trying to change your thinking and corresponding action, and consciously start speaking positively to yourself. Quit talking about how difficult it is, and try speaking about how exciting it will be when you start. Change those "if" statements to "when" statements. So instead of saying "…if I get an interview," and "if I get an offer" and start saying "when". Remember this feeling of "I can do it!" When discouragement comes, keep pushing on with the confidence that ultimately, you'll be smiling. Tough times don't last, but tough people do.

It is also important to check your affirmation statements. In other words, what follows "I" or "I am"? As you begin to pay attention to this, you would notice that you may have unconsciously trained yourself to declare some negative words to yourself. The truth is that, at any given moment, we are affirming something, as being a failure or being a success. As such, you should make sure your affirmation statements are positive and true to what you want to become. For instance, you should say "I am successful" and not "I am a failure" or "I am excellent" and not "I am average" or "I am punctual" and not "I am always late". I can't emphasise enough that the words that you speak from the abundance of your heart will eventually become your reality. So, watch what you are saying.

The story of a little boy named Rocky in primary school would help to bring this point to life. One day as his mum picked him up from school, the teacher explained to her that although Rocky was a bright kid, in a recent reading assessment, he had struggled so they had to make him repeat the class (as was the norm in that state). Rocky's dad came home to a sad wife, and on hearing what the teacher had said, he decided it was time for some home study and refused to accept the negative report. After a few attempts, he realised that shouting at the poor kid wouldn't work. Then, Rocky's mum decided to try something else; she thought if Rocky saw himself as a winner, even in reading, then he would start to improve. So, every morning when she dropped the kids at school, just before Rocky ran off with his sisters, she would call him back and say, "What's your line, honey?" His response was "I can do all things and be the best reader," and his mum would say, "What does that make you, honey?" To which he replied, "I am a winner, mum." As time went on, Rocky started seeing himself as a winner, and as far as he was concerned, winners should also be the best readers. After a few weeks, his parents had a meeting with the school, and his teacher said, "It is a miracle! His reading has improved dramatically!" She wanted to know what the parents had done. Rocky went on to win the reading award for his class that year. After he found out that the student ahead of him had only read three books more than he had, he decided to skip recess on the last couple of days of the school term in order to read more, and he completed five books in that time. When he was asked what happened, he said "I am a winner, so I had to win."

Are you a winner? In order to change your talking and thinking, start by doing something simple and new today. Take a piece of paper, write your future profile, what you want to achieve, and your idea of success, keeping in mind that the only limits are those that you place on yourself and those that you allow others to place on you. Then, write a clear statement about what you will give in exchange for this future. This can be value to your employer/industry, a business service, continuous self-development, etc. Paste it on your wall and memorise these statements. Each day, recite them both as frequently as possible. What you read and hear on a daily basis will change your thinking, your speaking and thereby, your present and your future as well.

It's All About Your Attitude

The difference between successful and unsuccessful students, right from the application stage, all the way through to the internship and job offer, is in the positive mental attitude. Constantly expecting the best, the successful student sees the positive in everything. This positive attitude and enthusiasm is a source of confidence, and is loved by employers. Simply put, your attitude towards the world (and everyone in it) determines the world's attitude towards you. So, if you are looking for a positive response from employers, start having a positive attitude. Thomas Jefferson said, "Nothing can stop a man with the right mental attitude from achieving his goal; nothing can help the man with the wrong mental attitude." If you aren't one already, you must learn to be an optimist; it is better for your health and increases your chances of success. For every bad thing that happens, find two things to be thankful for. For every rejection, there will be another opportunity. Yes, see it as a chance to improve yourself and give it another go. Again, your attitude really does make all the difference, as a positive attitude makes you more productive, more creative and more fun to be around. As a result, you will get the job you want.

Having a winning attitude helps you overcome temporary setbacks on your way to the top. In 1922, former U.S. President Harry S. Truman, at the age of 38, was in debt and unemployed much like the majority of students. Twenty-three years later, in 1945, he had become the most powerful man in the world, as the President of the United States. If he didn't have a positive attitude and persistent belief in his potential, then he wouldn't have attained such great heights in his career. Like him, we can benefit by viewing failures and rejections as temporary. Individuals with a poor attitude tend to internalise failure and take it personally. They often see failure as permanent, rather than having a positive attitude that says, "I failed at something, but I am not a failure." Zig Ziglar says, "Failure is an event and not a person." In life, we will all have an opportunity to say either "I missed that one," or "I am a failure," and those who choose the former are those you will find at the top. John C. Maxwell, in his research on successful individuals, concluded, "I think it is safe to say that all great achievers are given multiple reasons to believe they are failures. But in spite of that, they remain positive and they persevere. In the face of adversity, rejection, and failings, they continue believing in themselves and refuse to consider themselves as failures. They chose to develop the right attitude about failure."

I am sure that, as you read, you can think of people you know who, in your opinion, have a poor attitude and others who are more positive. Choose one person for each of these categories, and evaluate their attitudes. Then, consider how their attitude affects their performance and progress. I recently did a review of my attitude and then assessed my thoughts by asking friends to describe in one or two words what sort of attitude they thought I had. Responses included a "teachable attitude" (always willing to learn), "cheerful and outgoing", "disciplined", "extremely positive", "determined with no limits" and "upbeat".

When I asked my friend Abi to explain what she meant by "upbeat", she said, "No matter the weather, your focus and positivity are clear. Uche isn't working, so what? Uche is being more focused and diligent than some of his employed peers. Uche is preparing himself for his next role by keeping sharp as a knife, and that is upbeat. It is much easier to wallow in self-pity than to focus on self-development. It is much easier to binge than to write a book. That is upbeat." I haven't always been this way, but once you realise that, with a bad attitude, you don't need anyone to keep you from rising to the top because you'll do that by yourself, you quickly learn to adopt a positive attitude. I encourage you to do the same, considering the crucial impact of our attitude on our future success. Research shows that the reason a person gets a job and gets ahead in their job has more to do with their attitude than their technical knowledge; however, be sure to ask only those friends who will tell you the truth and not those who just say what you want to hear.

Keep Applying

To get that offer, you must keep at it. While some students are blessed and seem to get called for interviews after little work, others (like me) weren't so lucky. In such cases, you must keep applying until you have an offer or until you just can't anymore (e.g. every possible deadline is closed). As I mentioned, I applied everywhere, even companies I wouldn't have considered initially. Trust me, after you have done a normal shift job (like I did the summer before my internship as a waiter), you quickly realise that beggars can't be choosers, the fire in your belly glows brighter, and you decide not to give up. The key word is 'hunger'. You need to be hungry; strike that – starving. The best example I have of hunger is how an old Jewish King (King David) describes his hunger for God. He says "As the deer pants and longs for the water brooks, so I pant and long for You, O God." As this thirsty deer runs for a stream of water, you can imagine its desperation; there is no stopping that deer. That's how hungry you must be. I was desperate; everything about me in my penultimate year at university was focused on getting an internship. You need to feed your hunger – read, visualise what's possible, speak to those already living your dream and finally decide that you are not going to give up. I can confidently say that hungry people end up being successful, provided they remain hungry and don't get full.

We all have ideal situations in our mind about what we want and how we are going to get it. In my case, I was going to apply to my top five choices, get invited to interviews by all, and pick the one I wanted from all the offers I received. After all, I was in a good university, I was the VP of the Afro Caribbean Society, and I had decent work experience. But contrary to my expectation, I got rejection after rejection (fall after fall). So, I picked myself up and cheered myself on. I had a very clear picture of what I was aiming for, and nothing – absolutely nothing – was going to stop me. Things only really begin to happen when you decide that, no matter what happens, you are going to keep pushing onward. It is not enough to make a decision; your decision must be backed with action and commitment to improving yourself and, as a result, your chances. So, with each rejection, I got whatever feedback I could, made adjustments and tried again. It is easy to gloss over this last point, but it is key. It is often said that a crazy person is someone who does the exact same thing, but expects a different result. Based on that definition, I would certainly have been mad if I had thought I could do exactly the same thing in my applications (e.g. use the same answers) and expect to get invited to an interview. As simple as this sounds, many students fall into this trap of copying and pasting the same answers that got them their last rejection email. At least make some adjustments, after using the career advisory service and asking other successful students for guidance.

Let me make a quick point about how vital it is to surround yourself with the right people. Charlie Jones, the well-known author and speaker, certainly spoke the truth when he said, "The difference between whom you are today and who you will be in five years will be the people you spend time with and the books that you read." Spend some time evaluating your circle of friends and acquaintances. Do you have people who believe in you and encourage you to be your best? Your future is too important to be thrown away by hanging out with the wrong people. Think about who needs to come into your inner circle and who needs to leave. There is room to keep those acquaintances and people you might spend time with, but be careful who you let into your inner circle. Always ask yourself, "Are the people I'm following going where I want to go?" If not, you know you have some reshuffling to do, and please do it quickly. Below, I share how my friends and I got offers, but in hindsight, it was no surprise. We were all driven, willing to pay the price, and convinced that we had what it took.

If awards were given for the most rejections achieved, I would certainly have been a strong contender, so please don't think that the world is against you or that recruiters are evil. Rather, improve on your last attempt and try again. Psychologist Simone Caruthers said, "Life is a series of outcomes. Sometimes the outcome is what you want. Great. Figure out what you did right. Sometimes the outcome is what you don't want. Great. Figure out what you did so you don't do it again." Similarly, there is the story of a lumberjack who went out at the beginning of the week to cut some trees and came back that same evening excited with his results. By the end of the week, though, he hadn't made much progress, even though he worked harder every day. He came home grumbling to his wife about the poor results, wanting to give up, but she said, "Don't give up; you haven't sharpened your axe edge all week." A lot of people are like this lumberjack – they complain of not breaking through, but they fail to change anything on their next attempt. I really wish I could give you my resilience, but until scientists figure out a way to make that happen, please draw inspiration from those that have gone before you and keep pushing. This point doesn't only apply while you are in the application stage, but also during your internship. There will certainly be times when you fall, but that isn't the end – it isn't over until you have your job offer in hand.

The issue is not whether or not there are setbacks, but what we do when such setbacks occur. Successful people pick themselves up and keep moving, but the mediocre wallow in self-pity and give up. No matter who you are, in this life, there will be many trials and setbacks. The only difference between successful people and the rest of the world is in their response – they pick themselves up and give it another go, coming out stronger in the end. It is a proven fact that most successful business people have had at least two or three failed attempts, but guess what – they tried again. Just in case you're wondering how long you should keep trying, let's take a leaf out of Thomas Edison's book. We owe a lot to Edison. He knew in his heart that he could invent the light bulb, and with his assistant, he tried again and again after each failed attempt. After so many failed attempts, his assistant voiced his frustration and wanted them to give up. In the end, he had made over 10,000 attempts before he finally broke through, and today, we have the light bulb as the fruit of his efforts. A famous quote from Edison gives us an insight into his mindset: "If I find 10,000 ways something won't work, I haven't failed. I am not discouraged, because every wrong attempt discarded is another step forward." You see the only difference between Thomas Edison and his assistant was his ability to try again, plus his positive mental attitude. So, for how long will you keep trying? Until you make it!

If you cast your mind back to when Barack Obama lost the New Hampshire primaries in his run to win the US election, everyone thought it was over for him, but no, he and his team went back to the drawing board and tried again. I can't stress enough the importance of trying again. It is, in my opinion, one of the main keys to success in life – refusing to quit. You may have been unlucky, but don't quit. You may have been rejected, but don't quit.

Widen Your Search

To get as many offers as possible, you need to widen your search. While focus is necessary and good, if you don't get into McKinsey, for example, it's better to spend the summer in a small consultancy firm than to spend it as a shop assistant. Widening your search increases your chances of receiving multiple offers, which can also give you leverage. It is simple, just as the grass always looks greener on the other side; organisations always want what's good for their competitors. So, if you have an offer from Company A, guess what, you've gone from looking like a 65-year-old granny to looking like Halle Berry in the eyes of Company B.

The best example of someone who not only refused to give up, but also remained hungry and spread her net far and wide is my partner, Vona. By the time I received my offer, most of my colleagues had received offers – one of the lawyers had hers, the other economist had an offer, and the two engineers had their offers. Vona, the accountant, however, didn't have an offer, and we added salt to this wound by constantly discussing how much fun we'd be having over the summer with all the cash we'd all be earning. Despite all this, and rather than wallowing in self-pity, Vona pushed on, and with each rejection, she pushed even harder. Necessity, they say, is the mother of invention, and Vona proved it. She came up with companies I had never heard of and deadlines that we all thought had passed but had not. When you are keen like Vona, you just find a way. By the time internships were about to start, Vona had put us all to shame. She had three offers, can you believe it? This 19-year-old woman had three offers from three different companies: E&Y, ABN AMRO and Schroders Asset Management. As much as she wanted to become a chartered accountant, she went with the ABN offer – somehow £500 x 10 weeks made more sense than £250 x 6 weeks. Within months of starting her final year, she had permanent offers from ABN, E&Y, PWC and KPMG, who had rejected her back when she had applied for an internship. As I mentioned before, in these situations, competitors suddenly find you more attractive. She went with KPMG, her dream company.

Perhaps you always wanted to be an accountant, but then you only get an offer from an asset management firm. That doesn't matter; what matters most isn't where you start but where you end up. There are numerous examples of this. Sir John Bond, former chairman of HSBC, started off as a bank clerk. I've met some bank MD's who were qualified lawyers and some who were in the army; I've met accountants who now run restaurants, engineers who are now in strategy consulting, and the list goes on. I didn't start off in investment banking myself. After my many failed attempts to get in, the only shot I had was in corporate (relationship) banking. At the end of the summer, I had an interview with the investment banking guys in HSBC, and for what seemed like the hundredth time, I fell flat on my face. In fact, they actually told HR that there was no way I could work in investment banking and I shouldn't even be given an offer to join HSBC. I got rejected by every other company I applied to in my final year. I got interviews but they went nowhere. With support from my team, I finally got an offer from HSBC corporate banking for a place on their graduate programme. I could either give up on my dream of working in investment banking or I could keep the dream alive and keep pushing on. I often heard my brother say, "Where there's a will, there is a way," and it's true.

After a few weeks of working in corporate banking, I encountered an opportunity to work on a project in investment banking for one month. Finally, my time had come, and I could prove myself. By now, I was used to having only one shot and maximising it. My plan for that month was to make sure that the investment banking team I worked in saw my passion, and that I had what it took. In essence, I was still on an internship, and I strived to live by the tips I am sharing in this book. I learnt fast, worked hard and passionately, and made it my personal responsibility to lead the project to success. I always wanted to know if we were on the path to meeting our target, and what I could do to ensure that we did. I went from working 9 am to 6pm to working 8 am to 2 am. I was on a mission, determined to do whatever was necessary. By the end of the month, I had become one of the guys and the team were sad that I had to leave. On my last day, I was the happiest analyst alive. The director I worked with had asked if I wanted to come back because he was willing to speak with HR to ensure I did a rotation with his team or business area. When I got back to corporate banking, I maintained the work ethic I had gained while working in investment banking. I maintained dialogue with the guys in investment banking, and the only thing left to do was to wait patiently until the end of my corporate banking rotation.

That's when the fight began. HR didn't want me to go into investment banking for my next rotation, and they gave every excuse in the book. I didn't sit down thinking "This is unfair. Why me? Why can't things just work out?" No, I realised that life isn't fair, and you don't get what you deserve but what you fight for. By myself, I could do nothing, but I had backing and was going to maximise it. I found out that when you are excellent, people are willing to fight for you, and if you want to get ahead in any profession, you need senior management support. When my corporate banking MD and the investment banking director found out what HR was up to, they simply ignored HR and went straight to the head of the investment banking team to tell him that I was a great guy and I wanted to work in his team. Sadly, there was no opportunity in the team with which I did a one-month stint, but there was an opportunity in another team closely aligned to it. Was I interested in the team? At the time, I wasn't sure because it was all new to me, but I had learnt how to use what I had in order to get what I wanted. Everything began rolling like a wheel in motion.

The other team wanted to interview me. I felt like an intern all over again and remembered how excited I was, that thrill of preparing for an interview that could lead to the opportunity of a lifetime. The interview was more of a meet and greet. The MD of the new team kept talking about the praises I had received from his colleagues, and how he also perceived my diligence because he had sat close to me during my one-month stint. I picked up on the other secret – perception is everything; I accepted the offer and sat back. They took my battle from me. They told HR to ignore their plans and to get with the programme. It was simple – they needed a graduate, I was interested, and they wanted me because they knew what I was capable of. Reluctantly, HR agreed.

Was my dream finally coming true? First, a month and now a six-month opportunity? Would I be able to do it? One month had been a challenge; now, I had six months to prove myself. Quickly, I decided that I was up to the task. "Excellence" was now my motto because "Excellence is not a skill, it is an attitude." My game plan was simple – if you're going to succeed, you must have an 'intern mentality'. I hit the ground running and worked hard. I set myself a list of targets that I needed to meet and areas where I needed to demonstrate that I had the know-how. My mindset had to change from "me" to "we" (i.e. I kept thinking, "How can we, as a team, make it, and what part can I play?"). I always wanted to know why, and I never accepted the response of, "This is just the way it is." And when I found out why, I would go back to my desk and think of alternatives before bringing it up again. That way, I fully understood the issue. I knew I was on my way to success when, one day, a director was talking about an asset that would be difficult to finance, and immediately, I went on the net to begin research, even though she wasn't talking to me and hadn't asked me to do anything. She looked at my screen, saw what I was doing, smiled and said, "I simply can't leave you idle can I? Keep it up, you're doing well." I thought, "Perception, perception, perception is everything."

My plan had always been to wait until the end part of the rotation to let my team know I was keen on remaining in investment banking. But to my surprise, by the fourth month, another director asked me if I wanted to stay in investment banking. Not wanting to give my desperation away, I said yes with a smile, then ran out and started jumping. It was within reach, I was going to be an investment banker permanently. Next thing, the MD called a meeting and asked if I would please stay on. I quickly pointed out to him that I had one more rotation to do in corporate banking and that HR would certainly not allow it. He smiled and said, "Well, I will just have to offer you a permanent job then, won't I?" I couldn't believe it, I was being offered a job within four months on the desk. That must be a record, I thought, I had never heard of anyone doing that before. As usual, HR kicked up a fight. HR is great, but they don't like their plans being messed with. HR cried, "He can't be made permanent, he has been in the bank only 10 months, and he can't be promoted now." Again, I sat back and let my MD battle it out for me. I had learnt the secret a few months before – have senior management buy in, and there is no stopping you.

After a battle, HR conceded, and the result was that I would be transferred from the corporate banking programme to the investment banking programme and do my final rotation in the same team. That way, I could become permanent but still remain an analyst although that title, being short-lived, would be my next challenge. No one who heard what had happened could believe it. Most of the graduates in corporate banking desperately wanted to know how I did it. My answer remained consistent: "You must have an 'intern mentality', you need to genuinely want it, and must never give up." It is how I made the transition that I want to share you with you below. I didn't believe them when the bankers said, "You won't cut it" or when HR said "Don't bother." Little did HR know that, in a couple of years, they would be calling me to speak to interns on how to succeed in the bank! When people say you can't, don't argue with them, just remember that success is the best revenge. So, don't worry about those who have counted you out; just focus on achieving your goals.

My motto is simple – it isn't over until you get what you want. I once heard the story of a woman who had joined an investment bank as a secretary on the equity derivative desk, but eventually became an MD on the desk. If you prepare and work at it, there is no doubt that you can breakthrough and succeed. Often, I have asked myself, "Why do people give up and settle for less than their full potential?" I always come up with the same answer: "People give up because they have an acceptable alternative. If they didn't, and if the decision were a life-or-death matter, then they would keep at it until they broke through." The story of a trapped rat helps illustrate this point. While scurrying around one day, looking for food, this rat got trapped in a hole along the road, and every attempt it made to escape was in vain. In no time, the good Samaritans came to help the rat escape, but after many failed attempts, they gave up and offered to help find some food for the rat because it looked like it would be there for a long time. The rat agreed, and they headed off to find some food. Not long after they left, they heard the rat scurrying behind them. Shocked they exclaimed, "What happened? We thought you couldn't get out!" The rat replied, "Yes, that's true, but soon after you left, I heard a car heading in my direction, and I just had to get out." We break through only when we are trying to escape a desperate situation, but as long as the available options are acceptable, we will settle or give up.

Before you know it, the high of receiving an offer will be overshadowed by the magnitude of the coursework that's due and the exams that are just around the corner. If you ever wonder why the pressure seems to intensify towards the end of your penultimate year, I have the perfect analogy. Imagine you're the pot nicely set on a gas cooker, and the lecturer is in control of the knob. What do you reckon happens when the lecturer finds out that you're one step closer to getting a job where your starting salary will be equal to, or higher than his? You guessed right, that knob is going to get cranked up all the way, all for your good. So, between the offer and your starting point, your life is going to be overshadowed with coursework and exams. All I can say is, "Enjoy it, and give it your all!"

Chapter 5

The Awesome Four: Ways To Persevere

Matilda

By the end of the academic year, everyone had started reaping the dividends of their hard work, or lack thereof. It sometimes feels like, after a spell of bad news, good news starts coming through, like that's nature's way of testing our resolve. I got a phone a call from Matilda one day and she was so excited, she was screaming on the phone. She had been invited to two interviews! By the time the first interview date came, Matilda was well prepared. She didn't get the offer, and she was disappointed, but her second interview was a few days later and she was extra prepared. The next time Matilda called me, it was with good news. She couldn't wait to blurt it out – she got the job! It didn't matter to her that this was a lower-ranking law firm in the league tables; she knew this was the start of something great.

Fatima

Meanwhile, Fatima's networking was paying off. I called her just before she met with her new contact from Barclays Capital (BarCap), and I was surprised to find out that she was studying. Although it wasn't an interview, she didn't want to go unprepared. After the meeting, she was even more excited; her contact had agreed to recommend her to HR and had given her tips on how she could improve her application. With her new, improved answers, she applied to Barclays Capital and a few others. As expected, she was invited to the BarCap interview Fatima had already been preparing for a while, so when it was time for the interview, she was only solidifying her knowledge and had done a few mock interviews with her contact.

After the interview, she was buzzing – it was great, all the tips he had given were very helpful, and she couldn't stop going on about Barclays. Shortly after, HSBC invited her for an interview, and she was even considering skipping the HSBC interview because she believed Barclays was a done deal. So, you can imagine how distraught Fatima was when Barclays called her and gave her the bad news. When we spoke, she was clearly upset, but the disappointment had spurred her on, and she prepared extra hard for the HSBC interview, which she now had no choice but to attend. After that interview with HSBC, Fatima called to tell me how awful it had been. "It couldn't have been worse, they were mean!" She said. She was so upset that she hung up on me. Although she had been disappointed with how the interview turned out, there was actually still a flicker of hope, so when they finally called her to offer her the job, she fell to the ground with relief on hearing, "It's Emma from HSBC, congratulations!".

Steve

Being studious, Steve was going around trying to find students who had been called for interviews by the banks that had rejected him. He thought if five banks rejected him then surely something was wrong with his answers. As he went about trying to improve his answers, he kept doing his research and came across the Sponsors for Educational Opportunities programme (SEO). As he learnt more about SEO, he was excited to discover that their aim was to get ethnic minorities into City law firms, banks and technology groups. He was invited to the SEO assessment centre, and although he felt that he had messed up on his grasp of the numbers in the case study, (especially in light of coming from a science background), it actually turned out that Steve was being too hard on himself. The case study interviewers from the SEO were very impressed with his analysis. They explained that, whereas they could easily help him with the numbers, they couldn't give him brains, which he had already proved that he possessed. They also commended his knowledge of the industry, which had inevitably come across as a result of his disciplined approach to reading prior to the interview.

Leke

Meanwhile, Leke was still being picky and taking his time with his applications. With each rejection that came in, Leke paid more attention to improving his answers on his application form. After a few more failed attempts, and a few more tweaks here and there, he was called for an interview at Deutsche Bank. Leke prepared extremely well and, during the interview, he impressed them whenever possible by sharing his views on various topical issues. I guess it paid to be a 'Jack' after all. The interview was mediocre, in his opinion, and could go either way, which was nerve-racking for him. He claims he wasn't anxious, but on the day the fateful call came, I was with him. We were just chilling when the phone rang, and when he heard "Deutsche Bank" and something about being offered the job, he was flying all over the place like a bird freed from a cage.

Beginning Right

Exams are over, the summer is here, and you're about to start a very thrilling, yet demanding, internship. Naturally, we all want our efforts to start well and end well, but unfortunately it doesn't always go according to plan, so it's important to keep our expectations realistic. Interestingly, a great start doesn't guarantee a great finish, and likewise a poor start doesn't necessarily mean a poor finish. What happened on the opening day of the baseball season in 1945 illustrates this point. The Milwaukee Braves played the Cincinnati Reds, and a rookie from each team made their debut. The Reds' rookie, Jim Greengrass, had an amazing start; he hit four doubles and helped his team win 9-8. The Braves' rookie had a less electric start; he went 0 for 5. Jim Greengrass is probably a name that most baseball fans don't know, but Hank Aaron, who had that unimpressive start, ended up becoming the best homerun hitter in the history of baseball. Aaron probably would have given up baseball altogether if he had based his expectations on how he started, or if he had internalised that initial failure. Knowing that he had what it took, he used the short-term disappointment to motivate himself to prove what he was made of. Like I said before, always remember that you truly have what it takes, and never forget that the only thing keeping you from your success is yourself.

Just before I started my internship, I was excited but doubtful. Finally, all the hard work was going to start paying dividends, both tangibly (cash) and intangibly (credentials), but I kept thinking, "What if I totally blow it?" Everyone, even those with no experience, felt it was their duty to stress how difficult and important this opportunity was. Phrases like "It's a 10-week interview" or "Your most difficult experience yet", put me to bed and woke me up. I agree it will be tough, and you don't want to blow it, but starting the internship scared does you no good. Doing each task with the fear that you might mess it up, or interacting with people as though you're walking on egg shells will hinder your performance and might ultimately cost you the internship. Below are a few pointers for dealing with this anxiety and making the most of the internship.

Enjoy Yourself

Before you start your internship, decide that you're going to enjoy yourself no matter what. This might be hard to believe when you think of the grilling you got at the interview, but you will have a more productive working life if you can love what you do and have a good time doing it. All through your internship, each member of your team would be asking, "Can I work with (insert your name here)?" They aren't asking whether you can do the job, they want to know whether they can work with you. In addition to assessing your technical ability, your team will also be asking if you're fun to be around, if you can take a joke, if you interact with people well, if you can manage external clients, and the list goes on and on. Several times, I've heard MDs say, "We can teach a person all the technical stuff, but we can't teach them how to be likeable, keen, driven and fun to be around." This point goes back to what I said about being a rough diamond – employers are looking for qualities they can work with and improve. A friend of mine is an example of this. At the end of her internship, her team and HR were uncertain about what division she was best suited to, but the head of the desk decided she would fit well in the firm because she is likeable, fun to be around and smart. They gave her the offer without knowing where she'd fit, but they decided that they'd figure out which division would suit her best as time progresses. Now, in case you don't know, that's extremely unusual in the City.

Extremes Will Get You Nowhere

A word of caution, please avoid being extreme. It's very irritating when an intern pretends to be "holier than thou", always trying to please everyone and acting like they can do no wrong. The smell is foul and can be detected a mile away. Don't get me wrong, being genuinely keen and willing to help is different from pretending to be all goody-two-shoes when you really aren't. Bear in mind, a lazy person acts while a hard worker is just himself. In case it hasn't occurred to you, we have more experience than you, and we have seen it all. We know when you're acting, and the more you try to act, the faker it appears. Again, be aware that communication is only seven percent words. So, if you're saying, "I'm really keen to learn and help," when you're being given work or when you're doing the job, your whole being (body posture, etc) may be passing on a different message.

I often tell interns that they can pretend for a little while, but sooner or later, who they really are, deep down, will become apparent. So rather than act, let diligence, enthusiasm and passion be the real you. I remember an intern who appeared to be very keen, but after we caught her asleep several times – a sure 100-percent way of losing your offer – we began doubting how keen she was. And I'm talking about coming to get work, marching back to her desk in apparent eagerness to begin, and then promptly falling asleep with her head in her hand. You might think, "Come on, she was tired, that's a bit harsh, it can happen to any of us." I agree, but it's different when such an episode happens more than once, and also if that happens when, a minute ago, you were acting like you were super-interested, only to sneak away and sleep. So, what is the key? Don't be lazy, and prepare to work hard, so get enough sleep the night before.

Another extreme is when interns become too comfortable and forget: that they've only been with the team for a short period; that they don't have a job yet. One evening, I was in a car with a recruiter named Ken and a business representative named Xi, heading to a recruitment event, and we got chatting about factors that hinder an intern's success. In Ken's words, "A lot of interns start off well and soon forget that they're interns." When I asked what he meant, he said, "Some interns get too comfortable and begin acting like they've been part of the team for years. For example, some begin to swear because other members of their team do it or start gossiping to fit in. I tell you, Uche, some really shoot themselves in the foot." Xi concurred and gave similar examples of how students botched their golden opportunity by getting too comfortable and forgetting they were being assessed daily. Such interns begin to make expensive jokes and do things the way they think it should be done as opposed to how they have been asked to do it. Let this be your golden rule: when it comes to work, first do what you've been asked to do, and then add or improve the work as you see fit. If you suddenly get a brainwave and you know a better way of doing the piece of work, first run it by the person that gave you the assignment and leave the decision up to them. They might have a particular reason for wanting what they requested. When you're out and about with the team, it is important not to get too comfortable; don't forget that while they are your team mates they are also your potential employers, not your friends from university.

This is particularly important if you drink. There was once an intern who, being smart, hardworking and impressionable, got the offer, only to throw it away because he got too comfortable. Talk about things changing in the space of hours! In the afternoon, he was given an offer, and the following morning, the offer was rescinded. Why? Because at the dinner held for interns that evening, he got so drunk he ended up asleep (and I am talking about face-in-plate fast asleep) at the table with his team, after being a bit of a nuisance. Naturally, the head of the desk said, "It's one thing to be drunk, but it is quite another to pass out at the table." They couldn't afford to have such things happen with clients, so the offer was taken back. That underscores the point that, more than anything; employers are always looking towards the future.

At the other extreme, some interns are just too serious when it comes to work; it's as though they believe that it's a sin to have fun while they're at work. They're simply unable to mix work and fun; it must be either one or the other, and if they must choose one, it would be work. So, don't be pretentious, don't get too comfortable and don't be too serious – just aim to be in the middle and you'll be fine.

Putting Things In Perspective

What would you do if you had three months to live? Most people would decide to live life to the fullest and make the most of the time they have left, right? They become fearless. In like manner, remove that ultimate fear of receiving no offer, but do this with the advice of King Solomon in the back of your mind, "Whatever your hands find to do, do it well," and decide to make the most of the internship. Knowing that your reputation precedes you wherever you go, and that you are just one recommendation away from living your dream, give it your all.

Assuming that there was no offer, think about how you can maximise the internship. Spend time networking and forging relationships that will be instrumental throughout the life of your career. During the internship, learn as much as you can, and strive to become every employer's dream. In essence, there's so much to be gotten out of the internship itself, aside from the offer. Try to consider the offer as the icing on the cake; and don't miss out on the cake during your internship, because if you do, there will be no offer.

Chapter 6
Day 1

Sooner than I expected, the first day finally arrived. Crammed into one of London's infamous underground trains, I recited all the rules in my head, "Firm hand shake, eye contact, have those introductory lines ready…" I was petrified, and as I mentioned earlier, this is not the right state to be in. The first day was an anticlimax. It was like a promotion night when the boxers who will be competing for the title are weighed. In some cases, HR thoughtfully organised a dinner or drinks reception before the internship actually began. Whatever the case, all the interns were weighing each other up and trying to assess the competition. Although there isn't any exchange of insults (unless you can mind-read and hear what's really being thought), knowingly or unknowingly everyone tries to intimidate each other, mentioning what university they're in, their degree, how many other offers they got, etc. It's simply a battle of minds, and by the end of the day, you'll either be feeling great or feeling like you've lost the internship from the word 'go'.

The key is to win the battle like I did before the internship starts. How? I was fully aware that there would be people who had received multiple offers, who came from better universities, and who were even better-dressed than me. Knowing this, I prepared my mind and simply thought, "Despite all the achievements and expensive suits, we're on the same internship, earning the same amount, and we all have one thing in common – we're in need of a job, so may the best person win." Often, you will be tempted to fight back with sarcasm, as when John says, "I got five offers," you may want to say, "Wow, that's great, too bad you can only be in one place at a time." Or when Susan says, "I've already done two internships," you may bite your tongue to keep from saying, "And you're still interning? Life is tough, isn't it?" My advice is don't do it; this is a good opportunity to make friends, not enemies.

It is essential to be clear and convinced about this truth – the internship offer, like the application, only serves as a door. In other words, when you're invited to an interview, each student has exactly the same chance, irrespective of how good or bad your application was. Likewise, once you have the internship offer; all have the same chance of getting that permanent offer. As simple as this may sound, the reason why many don't excel is because their focus is split; there are two fights going on simultaneously – the fight to get a full-time offer and the fight in their head over the possibility that their bosses perceive the other students to be better. Whether this fearful mindset focuses on what university they attend, their level of experience, or their academic record, it creates additional pressure that can be detrimental. It is said that a "double-minded man is unstable in all his ways."

Even the best performers in any sphere of life will perform below par when they are not focused. To take an extreme example, imagine Michael Schumacher driving on an F1 circuit and using the phone at the same time. Even with the best will in the world, he'll come in last because even though he was the best in the world, the other drivers are pretty solid as well, and the slightest mistake by any driver on the circuit drastically reduces their chances. I was recently cruising down the streets of east London with a friend and became so engrossed in our conversation that I didn't realise the traffic light ahead had just turned red and I was heading directly towards the car in front of me!

Just in the nick of time, I swung the steering wheel to the right, barely missing the car in front. If any car was coming from the right, that would have been it, but for the grace of God. What's the point of this story? Many have crashed simply because they have believed a lie – the lie that they are not as good others due to the university they attended or the lie that, since it's their first shot at an internship, they have more to prove. Wake up from your slumber now or a crash awaits you! You are a star, and you will succeed. Yes, your university may be ranked 100th in the country, this may be your first time in a real professional environment, and you may be young, but don't sweat it! You have the same shot at success as every other intern, and by the end of this book, you'll know how to excel.

And just so we kill this issue of university ranking once and for all, I want you to picture the first day at one of the top-ranking universities in the country. You have students from all over the nation – the private-schooled, the government-schooled, students from the east and west, north and south, everybody. Though they come from very different backgrounds, they're all in the same university and there's no denying that they all have a good chance of finishing at the top of their class if they apply themselves. The top-ranking institution, in your case, is that City law or consulting firm, bank, or whatever else tickles your fancy; have people from different backgrounds, and each has a shot like you. It doesn't matter what preceded your internship; you all have exactly the same chance to make a real go of it.

Diversity Is Beautiful

Being a woman or an ethnic minority has deprived many from achieving their dream, despite the fact that we have seen many succeed irrespective of gender or race. As it was a problem for me and a few friends, I can only assume that some of you might have the same struggle, it is necessary to dispel the myth that your race or gender has anything to do with the likelihood of your success. For me, it was being black. For a long time, I sincerely believed that I had a slimmer chance of success and that I had to work twice as hard to prove myself. My saving grace was that Jeff, one of the directors in my team was a black American. In my opinion, if Jeff was a director, then surely it was possible to at least get a full-time offer. My confidence increased when I realised that the woman who sat a few desks away from me, was not only an MD but the head of an entire sector.

I could have had black and female MDs all around me, but if my thinking didn't change, then my chances of getting an offer would have been greatly reduced, and I certainly wouldn't be where I am today. Whatever you believe, is real to you. John Lilly put it beautifully when he said, "In the province of the mind, what one believes to be true either is true or becomes true." So, if you believe you are limited by your race or gender, you will be limited. The fact that what you believe (be it the truth or a lie) is real to you, is further proved by our phobias. In your life and work, you have enough things to keep you busy and to worry about, so there's no need to believe lies that limit you and put you under unnecessary pressure. Sometimes, the popular saying, "Seeing is believing" actually isn't true. You will be held back on your journey to the top if you believe that you are restricted by factors you have no control over, such as race or gender.

Everywhere you look, you find examples that destroy this myth. Zoe Cruz, married with a child, was the president of Morgan Stanley. Stan O'Neal, a black man, was the CEO of Merrill Lynch. Vikram Pandit (Asian) was the CEO of Citigroup. Baroness Scotland of Asthal, a black woman, was the Attorney General for England, Wales and Northern Ireland. Back in 1997, Marjorie Scardino was Pearson's first female CEO, and even the FTSE 100 added to their ranks Prudential's first black CEO, Tidjane Thiam, originally from Côte d'Ivoire. As you can see neither colour nor gender will hinder you, or at least it shouldn't, and yet so many people allow it to.

You must be clear that you have exactly the same chance as everybody else. Mr Thiam put it nicely when he said in a Times Online interview, "I just cannot see myself as a minority – I see myself as a human being. If you start wondering, when something happens to you, whether it is because you are you or whether it is because you are a minority, life becomes very complicated." I believe this statement summarises the mindset of the various successful people we have discussed and the way in which we all should think.

As I said earlier, you must renew your mind and get rid of any thoughts about your potential being hindered because you are a woman or from an ethnic minority background.

This topic wouldn't be complete, though, without giving tribute to the most inspirational story I have ever heard regarding this false mindset. It is about a young man who worked on the trading floor above the floor where I worked. He was not only an ethnic minority, he was also severely disabled and required a wheelchair for mobility. Yet, despite his disability, he not only succeeded in his internship, he was one of the few that didn't lose his job in the recession.

The longer I've been in the City, the more certain I've come to believe that the extent of your success is commensurate with how diligent and smart you are. And as for being smart, you can learn what you don't know, like I did. Not all of us are going to be chief executives, partners or presidents, as there is a price to pay and only a few are willing to pay it; however, don't sell yourself short by believing a lie. Decide what you want to be and how far you want to go. Count the cost, and if you're willing to pay that price, then by all means go for it.

Training

After the induction day, you may have a week of training. I won't focus on this too much, as only a few industries have this structure, and it really isn't a deciding factor in whether or not you get an offer. What I will say, though, is take it seriously and, at the end of each day, go home and do some revision to make sure that you grasp what's being taught. Training can be intimidating because some people seem to know it all, but if you actually do some work (like in university when you finally opened your dusty textbook), you quickly realise that they're not so smart after all; they just studied and applied themselves.

The Politician's Way

Your internship is really an election process, where you are the candidate and your team and HR are the almighty electorate. Using the US election process as an example, during the primaries, multiple candidates come up wanting to represent their party in the national election and, initially, all have a good chance. However, as time progresses, and as the electorate sifts through each candidate's records and manifesto, the successful candidate is separated from the pack. Ultimately, the electorate is looking for the candidate that will best satisfy their needs. A candidate is successful when they demonstrate that they not only can meet these needs, but would also continue to do so. Simply put, your firm is looking towards the future for those who will lead tomorrow. Up until now, your manifesto (CV/application form) has sufficed and you've had your chance at the rallies (the interview) to convince them that you're the right candidate. Now you need to demonstrate that you're the person for the job.

Just before we delve into the challenge of demonstrating your eligibility, let's take a few tips from the election analogy because what makes a political candidate successful is akin to what makes an intern successful. First, you have to be confident or come across as confident; you must not let your nerves get the better of you. If you aren't confident in yourself, you will find it difficult to get your team to have confidence in you. If you think about it, you'll find that we are all drawn to people who are confident. Just as people are unlikely to vote for a candidate that is clearly not confident, so would you struggle to get the offer if you're not confident. In my case, I wasn't really confident, but I made sure to come across as appearing confident. You see, confidence is really an issue of self-doubt – you may think you can't do it, but others won't know that, unless you give it away. So, even though there were times I thought I couldn't do the job or simply lacked what it took, I masked it pretty well. Applying what I've learnt from people who appeared confident (the operative word being "appeared"), I answered and asked questions boldly, I stated my opinion clearly and precisely, and I made jokes during my down time.

Like I said, the operative word is "appeared"; a lot of the time, people appear confident, but when you dig deep, you discover that they're a can of nerves. It's like the way a duck seems to glide effortlessly across the water – cool, calm and collected – but when you look underneath, you see its legs flapping away as though its life depended on it. You can take solace in the fact that you're not alone, but my advice is that you take it a step further and grow your confidence, rather than pretending to be confident. Pretence is a risky strategy because the real you can show up when you least expect it. I grew my confidence to the point where I was bold and didn't have to pretend anymore. Below, are some steps that you could take, but as with everything else that I'm sharing in this book, you have to try it out and apply yourself in order to enjoy the benefits.

Firstly, your confidence is built with each task you successfully complete and with each piece of knowledge you gain. Ultimately, your lack of confidence comes down to a combination of two things – your fear of messing up and your concern about the job or opportunity. The latter is a necessary ingredient for success in any endeavour in life; you must care passionately about what you do and go for it as though your life depended on it. As for the former, there is always a chance that you could mess things up, but you reduce the probability of this happening by learning and acquiring knowledge in your field and knowledge about what is required of you. In simple terms, know your stuff and after you believe you know the ins and outs of something, go over it again – it can never be too much. Knowledge is absolutely key; the more you learn about your business area and industry, the better you will be at your job and the more confident you will become.

There is no need to reinvent the wheel, though – ask your colleagues what you can read to enhance your understanding of the business and, in particular, that of the desk you are working. Chances are they may have some training material and other pieces of work that have been done in the past. I love learning from successful people, so take time to read any material written by someone you admire in your industry. There are always good books to read, so ask for recommendations from your team and other experts in your field.

Confidence comes with practice, and although practice may not get you to perfection, it certainly brings you closer to it. For example, when I joined the bank, I did not know much about Excel and PowerPoint, but I practiced every day. I would take previous pitches my team had created in PowerPoint and recreated them myself, down to the last detail. When I was stuck, I would ask questions, which meant more brownie points for me. I did this outside of work hours because, naturally, I was busy during the day. I became an expert in no time and soon could even show others a few tricks. My manager thought I was a fast learner and dedicated. Take time to practice every day in any area you are not confident in, and soon you will be.

In the meantime, I'll teach you a little trick called "anchoring". Compile a list of past victories and times you were unstoppable and untouchable. Then, fully remember and relive these moments – i.e. see what you saw, hear what you heard, feel what you felt. Repeat this process for a few different victories, and while doing it, create an anchor – maybe clench your left fist as a reminder. And when you find yourself struggling with the nerves, fire your anchor. As simple as this sounds, it works because confidence is a state of the mind and it helps you to realise that if you were successful then, you can be now as well.

The second thing is that, like the politician, you have to fight to the end and not quit. No campaign is without its obstacles; likewise, it isn't going to be a smooth ride all the way though. In fact, it is likely to be a rocky ride. But like Obama, you have to keep on fighting until the very end.

Finally, start with the end in sight. It is worth mentioning that, to a certain extent, you have no real control over whether you will be off to a good or bad start once you hit your desk. For some people, they have a bad start and it's almost like they're being repaid for all the bad they have done in the past; and then for others, it's heaven on earth. Whatever the case, what really matters is the end. So, if you are off to a good start, I am happy for you, but don't get complacent or overly comfortable. On the other hand, if the world seems to be against you during your first few days, don't sweat it; you are still very much in the race.

Chapter 7

Your Desk

All suited and booted, I headed up to the 19th floor to meet my team. I quickly brought up some discussion about the training session and mentioned how it provided a general overview of basic skills and an opportunity to hear about other business areas. I also thought it would be wise to manage expectations as I didn't want them thinking that I was now fully equipped and knew exactly what to do. It's better for your team to initially think that you are at a certain level and then realise that you're good. From the first day, all I wanted to do was work and prove that I was the man for the job. I had my own idea of what being a successful intern looked like. However, success in the eyes of my manager was not necessarily the same, although there were some commonalities.

A good way to start is to ask your manager for a chat and discuss what, in his eyes, you need to do to in order to be successful (i.e. his definition of a 'successful intern'). Even if he doesn't say much, you still win because you would look very keen. While you aren't asking the question to look keen rather to ensure that, over the course of the internship, you demonstrate your suitability for the job by meeting his success criteria. A word of caution: be prepared to answer the same question eloquently if you are asked. Whenever you ask a question, you should have your own opinion as often if you ask a question, that throws people off balance or catches them off-guard, they may push it back to you and ask what you think. Asking a difficult question can easily backfire. So, be smart and ask questions that whoever you're asking will know the answer to; this way, they can feel smart. We will look at the issue of questions in more detail later.

The next step is to ask your team manager if there are any problems that you can help sort out while you are there. It could be automating a process or creating a database, but whatever it is, it means more work for you because it will be in addition to your normal day-to-day job. If there is nothing, then as time progresses, look for any opportunity to add value. When I did my internship, the project I worked on was instrumental in securing my offer.

Collaborative Skill

If you haven't already found yourself in front of interviewers trying to prove that you are a team player, then at some point you will. I use the word "prove" because, if you aren't a team player, your chances of getting that job offer reduces. We are forever in one team or the other, from our family to sports or group projects, so we all have experiences (good or bad) of being part of a team from which we can learn. Just as being a successful team player is a prerequisite for success in these spheres of life, it is no different in a professional environment. If your team doesn't like you, you aren't going to be successful. If you have attended team-building courses, you've heard things like a, "good team player works to ensure the team as a whole is successful" i.e. your mentality is not how good you look, but how good we all look. Team players do not delight in the failure of other team members, nor do they seek to look good at the expense of others. When I heard things like that, I initially thought, "Yada, yada, yada, that's all nonsense", because I had seen people do crazy things to get ahead and felt I had no other option but to fight back with dirty tactics. However, in hindsight, I couldn't agree more that working for the good of the team is certainly your way to the top. Trust me, if you are diligent and do excellent work, you won't go unnoticed, and if you add to that a keenness to help other team members in whatever way possible, you inevitably make friends and can't help but succeed. It is important to take time to do a review of your collaborative skills and make adjustments where necessary. To accomplish this, ask those with whom you have worked on projects, played a sport or organised an event to give you some feedback. Also, think of those people whom you consider to be good team players and emulate the traits you admire in them.

Team Dynamics

Who's Got The Power?

It's important to be clear who has the decision-making power in your new family, as it isn't always the numero uno (head) of the desk or team. It helps if you know who you must score the most brownie points with and who you can't afford to upset. Think of your team as your family; after all, you'll be spending more time with them than with your real family. In some households, daddy has the final, and sometimes, the only say. This will be the head of the desk or team, like the MD or partner. In other households, daddy has the final say, but mum has his ears. This means that the real power is in the hands of another team member, not necessarily the head.

In one of my teams, this was the case – the MD surely had the final say, but the real power was with one of the directors. In this case, you had to ensure that you remained in the good books of two people. Finally, there is another case where there is a complete decentralisation of power. Here, you have family meetings to decide what's going to happen and everyone has a say. This means that, at work, everyone comes together to decide your fate. Naturally, some votes weigh more than others. Whilst it is good to be aware of these various styles, you should aim to be successful by acting as if your team has a decentralised approach, i.e. you should seek to be friends with everyone and remain in their good books. You want to aim to do something every day to help your colleagues and the people around you. Remember that your way up is to add value to your team by adding value to your co-workers.

No Hard Feelings

When I did my Junior O Level back in Nigeria, I remember how much I looked forward to the end of summer and starting my senior year because the tables had turned and I could enjoy the rewards of being promoted.

In Nigeria as a junior in state schools, you were at the mercy of the senior students. For example, a senior could stand up and shout "Hey, boy there!" and you will see a little army of junior boys running to the senior. The unlucky junior that was picked would be on errand duty. So, when you became a senior student, it was only natural that you fully exercised your rights. In like manner, when you get in, you are the answer to the prayers of the analyst or trainee, who is looking for someone to dump work on and take out their frustrations on. This will happen inevitably. First of all, it is good, as it gives you an opportunity to prove yourself, and secondly, you should simply see it as paying your dues. I remember the first intern that joined my desk. If there is anything he couldn't complain about, it was lack of work. Sometimes I dreamt up work for him to do, not because it was particularly necessary, but just because it was good to have. So, roll up those sleeves and get to work. Also, make sure not to ignore junior team members based on the assumption that they're unimportant to the recruitment decision. That is most certainly not the case as they are usually best placed to give you the most relevant insight into the role. Furthermore, they can be helpful when it comes to advice on people to network with and tips about do's and don'ts in relation to your team and the internship, as they've been there.

Danger Zone

I am the youngest of four kids, and I remember the good old days when my older siblings would come home frustrated and I was the one they'd take it out on. In those days, I would do everything I could to stay clear of danger. Your team will be no different. Take the associate who just got dumped by his girlfriend or the MD whose wife is nagging him – they'll be looking for any opportunity to let off steam. On such occasions, imagine that you're working in a minefield, so tread carefully. Also, don't act like you don't care and can't be bothered, ask if everything is okay. On one occasion, I didn't care and I showed it, and all it did was get the person more upset. Show some empathy and endeavour to stay clear of the danger zone. An email I once read explains what your attitude should be when colleagues are stressed out and taking it out on you or anyone else they can. It certainly changed my views and has helped me in relating with people, so here it goes; it is called "The Law of the Garbage Truck":

"One day, I hopped in a taxi, and we took off for the airport. We were driving in the right lane when suddenly a black car jumped out of a parking space right in front of us. My taxi driver slammed on his brakes, skidded, and missed the other car by just inches! The driver of the other car whipped his head around and started yelling at us. My taxi driver just smiled and waved at the guy. And I mean, he was really friendly. So, I asked, 'Why did you just do that? This guy almost ruined your car and sent us to the hospital!'

This is when my taxi driver taught me what I now call, 'The Law of the Garbage Truck'.

He explained that many people are like garbage trucks. They run around full of garbage, full of frustration, full of anger, and full of disappointment.

As their garbage piles up, they need a place to dump it, and sometimes they'll dump it on you. Don't take it personally. Just smile, wave, wish them well, and move on. Don't take their garbage and spread it to other people at work, at home, or on the streets. The bottom line is that successful people do not let garbage trucks take over their day. Life's too short to wake up in the morning with regrets, so ... Love the people who treat you right. Forgive the ones who don't. Life is ten percent what you make it and ninety percent how you take it!

Have a wonderful, garbage-free day!"

So, have a great time, and try to have a garbage-free day.

Characters

No two teams are the same, but more often than not, you will find a mix of characters. There is often the joker who makes everyone laugh and is fun to be around. These people are great to work with, but you must be careful not to get too comfortable or complacent around them. Be on your best behaviour even as you're friendly; don't risk getting a bad reputation by making expensive jokes, not placing priority on the work they give you, making silly mistakes you wouldn't otherwise make or asking simple questions that you could easily find out on Google. Instead, you want to maximise the opportunity to become friends with them and ensure they feel valued and respected.

Then, you have the stern colleague, who often leaves their sense of humour at home, and can be quite intimidating, even when giving you work. When you make a mistake, you certainly get an earful. With these people, you are guilty until proven innocent, i.e. you don't deserve an offer until you show you're worth it. When they call your name, you literally want to head for the fire exit. I often feel such people are trying to compensate for one insecurity or another. Whether that's true or not, I personally see it as a challenge, and I go the extra mile to prove that I am up to the task and more than worthy of an offer. You simply have to do your best not to step on their toes, and when you do (as you certainly will), remember that it will eventually pass.

Then you have those who are stern but nice, and you wish everyone could be like them. Interestingly, you are likely to perform above par on the jobs they give you because, in a strange way, you feel you owe them for being nice and believing in you and that you must not disappoint them. Whereas stern colleagues instill fear in you, people that are nice give you a sense that you can do it. One issue with these sorts of team mates is that you may get a false sense of doing well because they are forever nice. So, you may think you are doing great, while they're thinking that you're doing just okay or even below par – it can be hard to tell. The second issue is that when they give you work to do and you don't do it properly, they tend to sort it out themselves instead of asking you to redo it. You must manage them, ask for clear honest feedback and find out if you need to make any improvements to any work you do. You may be tempted to want to work with them only, but don't. Endeavour to work with and get along with all of the various characters on your team.

After all is said and done, there are some bad teams, and you have to make the most of it and remember everything you need to succeed is within you. Is that really true? Yes, because ultimately, if you are nice, well-liked and diligent, you will be just fine.

The Fruit Principle

Earlier, I spoke about attitude and how important it is to have an indomitable attitude, an attitude that says, "I won't give up, it might not have worked out as I wanted, I may have failed in that attempt, but one thing is certain – I am not a failure, and I will give it another go." But there is another important aspect of our attitude that is equally important, and I call it "The Fruit Principle". Imagine if you would, an apple. I want you to picture the best-looking apple you can. It looks so good; you can hardly wait to get a mouthful. As you pick it up, it feels just as good as it looks, and all that's left is for you to take that bite you've been imagining. But then you take the bite, and it doesn't taste great at all. We've all had moments when something we've craved for suddenly falls far below par with a most sour taste. That taste is your attitude. That bite could either have been great or nasty, and it actually determines whether or not you are kept and enjoyed or are dumped. It is people's perception of you. Are you a breath of fresh air and are people excited to see you? You might be wondering how do I know this, but believe me, if you take time to think and observe how others behave when you are around, you will begin to get a good idea about this. And as always, ask those close to you and who want the best for you, and they will be able to point out some traits that need changing. There are some attitudes you need to get rid of – for example, you shouldn't talk back to show you are tough. Being proud and acting as though certain tasks are beneath you, won't do you any favours. Whining and getting puffed up when things don't go your way makes you look immature, like a kid who has been refused candy. Engaging in back-biting as a form of defence will make you look bad.

Bad attitudes won't get you very far, people can easily tell when someone has a bad attitude, and they won't like being around them. You may look good and appear to have a lot of potential, but what do you taste like? Are you the apple that has the eater asking for more, or do you repulse the eater so much that they chuck you into the bin?

The other thing to beware of is that attitudes are contagious, and bad attitudes spread much faster than good attitudes. It is as though we doubt the good we hear about others, but are quick to embrace the message when it's something bad. When you start your new position, people often feel it is their duty to tell you what they think about other members of the team, but be careful because their positive and negative opinions can influence how you begin to interact with team members. Think for a second what happened when Fred told you how annoying Lucy was, and how you started seeing Lucy through the same eyes as Fred. You may be meeting Lucy for the first time, and she hasn't done anything annoying, but already you think she is a nuisance because of Fred's comments. Chances are Lucy may be cool, but you relate to her as if she were annoying. You want to be very careful; you don't know the history between Fred and Lucy or the reasons for his opinion. Endeavour not to take sides and aim to be neutral. Love everyone and be loved by everyone because we get back what we sow.

Vona was staffed on an audit job with a manager who she had never worked with before. When she told her colleague Jenny who the manager was, Jenny proceeded to tell Vona how that manager was very difficult to work with because of her micro-management style. When Vona started, she already had adopted Jenny's bad attitude towards her manager, and so she complained at the slightest opportunity. She started being abrupt with her manager and even wanted to tell her to back off and give her some space. Seeing what was happening, I told Vona quite plainly that she was being carried away because by reacting that way with this manager, she wasn't being Vona, but Jenny. Shortly after, Vona had a one-to-one with her manager, who couldn't stop singing Vona's praises to the director of the audit assignment, even after only a week of working and not doing that much. It turns out the manager on Vona's previous job had only good things to say about Vona, and her new manager simply saw Vona as the best. As they spoke, her manager gave her invaluable advice and was very willing to assist in whatever way she could to help Vona progressed in her career and in KPMG. By the end of the conversation, Vona's opinion had changed and she called me, telling me excitedly how her manager was great and a big supporter of her. Had Vona not given her manager a chance, she would have lost a valuable ally and could have ended up with an enemy. If you must be infected by someone's attitude, then make sure that it's a good attitude, a winning attitude and an ally-building attitude. And don't forget that bad attitudes compound faster than good attitudes, so beware.

Chapter 8

The Awesome Four: Guiding Lights

Steve

Steve continued his learning rampage before starting his internship. He felt that his science background would hinder him, and he wasn't going to let it. Websites were good for learning but, he needed more, and books were his solution. He read *Introduction to Capital Market, Liar's Poker and Monkey Business*. The more he spoke to bankers, the more he realised that if he was going to be successful, in addition to working hard, he would also need knowledge, the ability to relate with people effectively and some luck. Although he was fairly comfortable with his abilities, he intentionally set out to enhance his skills. He read *How to Win Friends and Influence People* by Dale Carnegie and practiced the tips he learnt in the book with friends. As for knowledge, he had that covered, and the only other thing he could do was pray for luck to be put in a good team. During his first week he was scared, and the culture shock had taken him by surprise. Luckily, his team were reasonable, and he had no problems settling in.

Leke

Leke was less lucky at first. When he started, his nerves got the better of him. He started to realise that if the future he saw was going to be a reality, it would come incrementally and only as a result of maximising every opportunity. In his new role, he stood out like a sore thumb. He didn't pay attention to how he dressed; his suit was pitiful compared to others' attire. On his third day, he was asked by Greg, a vice president, to do something, and Leke said, "I can't now I am doing some work for Ted." To which Greg replied, "It's okay. I am only a VP." Leke wanted the ground to open up and swallow him when he realised Ted was an associate and he had refused work from the vice president. So, by the end of the first week, Leke felt his start couldn't have been worse.

Fatima

Fatima set out to find someone willing to mentor her after realising how much she hadn't picked up during her training. She came across Hussein, a guy from another team who took her under his wing, as he was passionate about helping interns. Unlike other teams, Fatima's desk had two interns – Fatima and Thomas.

That wasn't a problem except for the fact that Thomas was the ideal candidate. He knew everything about everything; his dad and grandfather were both investment bankers, and he made the extra effort to show his knowledge whenever he could. Initially, Fatima thought the best way forward would be to cram stuff and spout out her newfound "shallow knowledge", but Hussein advised her otherwise. He said since things are quiet on your desk, look for the least-busy associate and learn as much as you can from him. Ask questions, review the answers, and then ask more questions. You would notice that he would become more likely to give you work when stuff comes up, and you would be showing that you are keen. So, Fatima set out to read all she could and asked questions. When she was given her first presentation task, she wisely asked Hussein to take a quick peek before submitting it. He pinpointed errors and advised her on how to improve it and when she submitted her first piece of work, she received valuable feedback and glowing positive comments.

Matilda

Matilda only had two weeks to prove herself, being on a law internship, which was practically over before it started. She thought the best way would be to play it safe, but as she later discovered, playing it safe can turn out to be a bad strategy if you play it too safe.

Transition

As I mentioned earlier, whether you have a good or a bad start is immaterial as your fate isn't decided on day one, but at the end of your internship. At the beginning, in the eyes of your team, you are just an intern; however, by the end of your internship, your aim is for them to see you as an analyst (using banking lingo). For them to see you as important, you would need to have successfully shown transition from being a student who is there temporarily to becoming a team member who is about to take a one-year sabbatical. Basically, after your internship, you hope they'll notice that you're not there. When I started my internship, I was as close to being an intern as one could get – I had no previous experience of working in a professional environment. When someone told me to add "Kind regards" at the end of an email, I realised how clueless I was. Though I had the internship, I couldn't write emails properly, and I was clueless in other ways. By the end of it all, my achievements included:

- Developing proficiency in PowerPoint and Excel.

- Writing a report that my team utilised to assess their approach to entering the European market.

- Single-handedly persuading a director in a research company to give me a copy of their research report for my sector that was not going to be publicly available for another few weeks, enabling us to get ahead of the pack.

If anyone ever told you hard work and determination doesn't pay, they lied!

So How Do You Make This Transition?

It's worth looking briefly at how not to make the transition. To do this, I will explore the habits of a colleague of mine before she was sacked. Just before I joined my team to start my six-month stint in investment banking,

Susan was being interviewed for an associate role. She eagerly accepted the offer, and my team sang her praises because she had impressed them during her interview and looked the part. Unfortunately, Susan, who was a smooth talker and a good dresser, was all talk and no action, which led to a bad review and, ultimately, the sack.

The first thing we noticed was that Susan very quickly developed the habit of "Last In First Out" (LIFO). It was okay for her to come in late a few times because of the trains, but other members, who, unlike her, had to commute from far, were still in on time. This habit quickly became noticed, and the senior guys started to lose their patience with Susan. Coming in late was bad enough, but often being the first to leave was very telling of her level of commitment to the team and the job. There were times she would leave even when others in the team had a lot to do and she could have assisted. To compound her LIFO habits, she started pulling sickies.

The second thing was that her word gradually lost meaning. Susan lied on more than one occasion. Sometimes, it was saying she had done something she hadn't or saying she thought a deadline was later than it was. Other times, it was lying about another team member thinking she could pull a fast one because they were on a business trip or holiday. The interesting thing was that although she thought she was being clever, the whole team knew she was lying and started placing little value on her word.

People even began to wonder if she had ever really worked in a bank before. Susan's work was usually poor. She was quick to finish, but speed loses value when your work is not up to par. It also testified to the fact that she was eager to leave early. Too many times, I saw a director angrily march to her desk to show her all the corrections she had to make and telling her to take her time. In no time, Susan was being given menial tasks that could afford to be messed up or not completed on time.

Despite all this, I still hold that if she had maintained a great attitude and controlled herself, she may have been tolerated and they may even have helped her with external time keeping and project management training. I've heard senior executives say over and over again that they would rather work with someone who had a good attitude and less talent, than someone who is very talented and has a nasty attitude. Susan would often speak under her breath and, more than once, she would openly debate with a director rather than express her views privately. The last straw was when she pulled a long sickie and said her GP had instructed her to take some time off. Naturally, she was asked to provide a letter from her GP, but when my team saw a photo of her partying on one of those days she was meant to be sick, Susan kissed her job good bye.

The Right Way

Over the years, I've learnt that the secret to becoming a successful person lies in your daily attitude, work ethic and habits. An interesting way of looking at it is like this. Dr. Sola Fola-Alade, author and publisher, says, "Seconds give birth to minutes, minutes to hours, hours to days, days to weeks, weeks to months, months to years and years to your destiny." In other words, what you consistently do daily for the duration of your internship (and life) determines whether you succeed. Although I have mentioned it earlier, it is important to still emphasise the significance of consistency. One of the traits of unsuccessful interns is that they are hot today and cold tomorrow in terms of their quality of work, attitude and enthusiasm. Being told that you did a good job on Monday, and then a reprimand to pay attention on Tuesday, only means you are back to square one. I'm not saying you'll always be in the good books, but you must strive to be consistently, and that boils down to hard work and discipline. The question is how badly do you want Success?

I have listed below the key attributes that make a successful intern, and these attributes, although not fully exhaustive, play a key role in your overall future success if *applied*. I emphasised "applied" because you might as well put down this book if you aren't going to bother applying the principles shared. As with anything in life, knowledge not applied is wasted knowledge. Do you ever wonder why an overweight person with a shelf full of books on losing weight and exercise DVDs is still overweight? It is simple – they lack application.

Make a commitment today to ensure that each day pays tribute to your ultimate vision and goal. Make each day count. Do something every day that brings you closer to your vision and the future that you want. Read a book, a journal, an industry magazine or any other relevant material. Become adept in MS Office suite. Put pictures of the future you want on the wall and ask what you are doing to get there. Many people want a brighter future, a dream job, a holiday in Hawaii and to be driven by a chauffeur, but only a few are willing to do what it takes.

Today, choose to be different and make a commitment to live your best life now. I remember the story of one of the most successful newscasters in the US. He grew up in the slums and, as a result, he didn't have the best educational foundation. He was able to get into university against all odds, and in his first lecture, he proudly proclaimed to the lecturer that he wanted to be a successful newscaster. The lecturer dismissed him and said he could never be one. Dejected and discouraged, he decided he was going to quit university. Luckily, on his way out, he met the Dean, who asked what was wrong and he described what had happened. Furious, the Dean suspended the lecturer, and convinced the young student to continue in university. The Dean also made sure that his roommate was a student from a more affluent background. When he met his roommate, he declared his vision again, but this time it was well received. Explaining that he would not become a newscaster with such a bad vocabulary, his roommate promised to teach him a new word every day. At the beginning of each day, he would get his assignment (a new word), and in the evening they would practice using the word in sentences. This went on for four years, and today our man from the slums is a huge success.

If you want to be successful, you need to dismiss the idea that you have the whole duration of your internship to prove yourself. A truly successful intern aims to make their mark by their midterm review. Granted, there are individuals who, after a poor midterm review, have gone on to be successful, but that is a risky strategy, and in our increasingly competitive job market, you should keep the risk of not getting a job to a minimum. Therefore, approach your internship as if you only have half the time to prove yourself. Remember that by your midterm review, your company is going to make the decision as to whether to make an offer – so plan to get an early promotion and achieve more in a shorter timeframe. Don't take little pieces of advice like this for granted because you only need to be slightly better to be in the top 10 percent of your intern class (and field) and to gain a competitive advantage.

Making The Transition

The first thing you must do is be clear about the role you are trying to transition in to. Because it is this understanding, coupled with the attributes listed below, that lead to promotion. Often you are promoted because you are already doing what an individual in the role above you is doing. So, as an intern, you should know:

- What does a successful analyst or trainee do? You must be clear about the responsibilities for your next level because it is only when you have demonstrated that you are able to handle these responsibilities (and more) that you are promoted.

- What does a successful analyst or trainee know? Just as knowledge and its application is the difference between the rich and the poor, it is also the difference between you and your next level. You have to be operating from the same knowledge base as those in the position you aspire for. Granted, it will be difficult to know the same amount as an analyst or trainee in your summer internship, but demonstrating how much you have learnt and your desire to continue learning will bring your promotion.

- How does a successful analyst or trainee behave? The question is, are you mature enough for the next role? Sometimes, you find an individual who is knowledgeable and who can certainly do the job, but the only drawback is that they need to mature. Although I accept that maturity comes with time, the simple truth is maturity is also a choice, and I believe that those who choose to mature will mature.

Chapter 9
Attributes Of Success

Diligence

Diligence is the constant and steady application of one's self to achieve a goal. Diligence is when someone asks you to go one mile for them, but you end up going two. It is doing over and above what is expected of you, a little further than others are willing to go. You have to give yourself completely to your tasks, as if each task were your only opportunity to prove yourself. Paul, in the Bible, advised his protégé Timothy to "give himself wholly..." In other words, you should refrain from being distracted during your internship, and should maintain a sharp focus so that your progress will be evident for all to see. It is your progress from the point you start to when you finish that determines your success. Diligence is Tiger Woods, who practices the same shot a hundred times; diligence is Cristiano Ronaldo, who is the first to arrive at practice and then stays two hours afterwards; diligence is David Beckham, who practices the same free kick a hundred times a day.

I once spoke to HSBC's global head of leverage and acquisition finance and, as usual, asked how he had become so successful. He said the most important thing is caring about what you do and taking responsibility for its success. He explained how he was never one of the smartest guys in the room and never got an MBA, but he was dedicated to the tasks at hand, always applied a common-sense approach and he couldn't over emphasise the need to prepare for everything, even for simple conversations. He said you must be confident in yourself, know that you're going to win, and don't look for people to fail so that you may look good. Be the best, irrespective of who is around. That is the mindset of a diligent person.

I have long realised that there is no point envying those who are successful because you have the secret within you – the ability to be diligent. Like King Solomon said, "Do you see a man diligent and skillful in his business? He will stand before kings; he will not stand before obscure men." Today, we see the reality of that statement, from the sports world to Wall Street; the best have had an audience with presidents and kings alike. It doesn't come by wishful thinking; it doesn't come because you are of a certain race or because you had it easy or tough growing up. No, it comes because you decided to give yourself wholly to the vision and goals/tasks along the way. Diligence results in skill, and it is the skillful that will excel. Solomon also said, "Whatever your hand finds to do, do it with all your might." Another tip from Solomon

"The hand of the diligent will rule, but the slothful will be put to forced labour." Many are doing jobs they would rather not be doing and wishing they could rewind time and start off diligently, but may feel that it is too late to change. If you strive to become diligent, you will rule in your field and stand before kings, and the words that will be used to describe you will be "reliable", "dependable", "consistent" and, of course, "diligent".

One day, I was thinking about inspirational stories of people who came from humble beginnings and became great. This got me wondering why anyone could fail when there is so much information on websites and books on how to succeed and get ahead in life. Finally, it dawned on me. Everyone has the same chance and access to the information, but only a few decide to be diligent, and it is that small group that earns 80 percent of the income. That's a reality of life, for example in Italy, in 1906, Vilfredo Pareto found that 80 percent of the land was owned by 20 percent of the population. You might be thinking that this is unfair, but please wake up and smell the coffee – this is a very common law of business. The bulk of profits, sales and exertion come from the minority, and it is this minority that enjoy the fruits of success. If the law of business is going to tilt in your favour, it won't happen by wishful thinking, it will only happen by diligence.

Early Riser

When most of the population are sleeping, successful people are up and working. One of the best pieces of advice I was given before I started my career (i.e. internship) was to be the first in and last out. I don't know about you, but when I was a student, that didn't come to me naturally. For me, it was more like last in, first out when it came to lectures, but I'm glad I took this advice. You must discipline yourself to wake up early. In the first week of my internship, I was quite surprised to find that the head of my desk got in before me and everybody else. Then, I tried to get in even earlier, and he still got in before me. What was even more interesting was that as I looked around the floor, the MDs of most teams were in before the rest of their team. Like I said above, successful people are willing to pay the price. The primary aim of getting in early is so you can get a head start over your colleagues. I must admit though, when I started coming in earlier, I only did it because I was told to and so that I would look very keen. Although I was in early, I would play on the Internet and only start working when most people had come in. I very quickly realised how much I was doing myself and the company a disservice and started to utilise my head start to finish work more quickly, to get more practice, to do research and to get closer to the MD.

Perceptions are important. During my midterm review, one of my line managers said, "When I come in, you are there, and when I leave, you're still there. Even if you weren't doing any work, I feel you are very hardworking." Now, he knew I was working hard because I met every deadline and asked for more work. But the point is even if I was not working "very" hard; his perception was that I was. Little did he know that on days when I wasn't very busy or when I was being lazy, I did a countdown and was out of the door shortly after he left! In fact, even if you don't have work to do, there is reading to do and skills to perfect. Sometimes you'll hear interns on their first week say, "I don't have much to do, so I'm going to leave early." I would think, "So you know all there is to know about the business, and there aren't any research materials to read?" It made them look lazy and uninterested.

Don't be like these people; apply yourself and you won't regret it. Even if your team says don't stay late, still leave last and work hard while you're at work.

Getting in early becomes a challenge when you have late nights out during the week. Remember you aren't in university anymore. Stumbling into work like you would in a lecture isn't very smart. My advice would be to leave the crazy nights for the weekend and stay focused during the week. You must always consider how you are perceived. You can be the best candidate, but if your team has the wrong perception, you won't get very far. Get a head start by getting in early, and maximise that time by using it to finish work quicker, read and practice. As you begin your career, always have it at the back of your mind that you want to be remembered for the right things.

Questions

When I joined HSBC, I had the opportunity to sit next to Sir John Bond when we had dinner with the management team. In my usual manner, I wanted to know the secret to his success. So, I asked what one main factor he would attribute his success to, and his response was interesting. He said, and I paraphrase, "If I am to pick only one factor, it would have to be being inquisitive." He explained how he always wanted to know why and how, and after he found out, he would probe even further. He wasn't enquiring in order to look keen. No, he was enquiring because he was genuinely interested. Being inquisitive is a must if you are going to be successful. Even after the question has been answered, take time to think it through and ask yourself further questions. Why is it this way, is there any other way it can work? The more inquisitive you are, the more you learn and the more you increase your knowledge. The more you know, the further you will go. Companies are looking for individuals with the potential and willingness to learn.

Before I started my internship, I learnt a golden rule of questioning from one of my mentors. When you ask a question, ensure you are asking the right question to the right person, at the right time. Questions are great, but effective questions must meet these three criteria. You can ask the best question ever to the right person, but if you ask it at the wrong time, you will get no benefit. With regards to who is the right person, it is likely that you can ask anyone on your team, but as you observe and learn more about each person, you will notice that certain questions are best suited for certain people. If a question relates to a certain piece of work, ask the person who gave you that work, not the person you are more comfortable with.

There are also questions that are generally suited for junior people on the team, i.e. the more technical questions. You should always remember that asking the right question also means not asking a question that you have clearly not given any thought to and especially not when the person is very busy. In your bid to look keen and interested, you can end up looking stupid, so be careful. For example, an intern met the MD of a team briefly while getting some coffee, and he quickly took the opportunity to ask if they could have a chat over coffee later on in the week. Very excited, he returned to his desk and decided to send the MD an email saying it was nice meeting him. However, in a bid to show his interest in the MD's team, he asked what sorts of tasks and hours the analysts do. It was no surprise that the MD emailed him back saying, "If you want to know what an analyst does, ask an analyst. Next time, think of who you're asking before you ask a question."

The second rule of questioning is to ask a question only once. The first thing you must do when you start is get a note pad, and whenever you ask a question, write the answer down. You won't appear smart if you ask a question twice, it simply does you no good. You might have a super retentive memory, but I like to write things down, so I can refer back to it. Also, the act of writing it down will reinforce it in your memory. To stand out, you are going to have to learn a lot quickly, so save yourself time and create space in your mind by writing answers down. Also, your note pad simply must be with you whenever you go for a meeting. You want to take notes always, and it gives you the ability to note down points that come up that you don't understand. I even take a note pad when I am meeting up with someone senior for coffee or lunch. This is my preference because I want to capture some pearls of wisdom, and it also gives the person a feel for how much I value their time.

Finally, take time to think about your question before asking it because you might be asked for your opinion, and if you say that you don't know, you will look as if you haven't thought about it all. Indeed, there will be some questions that you will have no clue about, and in those cases, you won't be expected to know the answer. If, in the process of thinking through, you realise you don't need to ask the question anymore, then you can say something like, "I had this question, and this is my understanding … is that correct, and is there any more light you can shed on the issue?" That way, you look smart and inquisitive.

Patience

One drawback I have seen in a lot interns is an over-eagerness to impress and they end up doing a lot of tasks in an average way rather than excelling at a few tasks. They ask for more work even before they have finished other tasks, thereby putting more pressure on themselves, and are unable to deliver. As your aptitude, talent and skill in the job increase, you will be able to do multiple tasks to a high standard. When you start, though, always have it in your mind that there is no substitute for excellence and no excuse for a mediocre job. You must simply learn to do things excellently, and this is less likely when your attention is spread over too many tasks to which you haven't become accustomed to yet. It is much better to do three tasks excellently than ten in an average way. Now, you might wonder, "How do I say no to work?" I am not advising you to say no to work. All I am saying is, when it comes to deadlines, manage yourself and the expectations of your team effectively. For example, if someone asks if you can help out with some work while you are already busy, say that you would love to but have to finish something for Mr Joe by a specific time and ask if it's okay to do their job afterwards. Be careful, though, if the person asking is senior to the other person whose job you're already working on. In that case say, "I can start yours now, but would you kindly tell the other person that I've been asked to put a hold on their job?"

While managing your deadlines, you have to work with speed and accuracy, but don't put yourself under undue pressure by agreeing to do too many things without renegotiating the deadlines. A lot of interns say yes to everything because they are desperate to prove themselves and/or afraid. In the process, they often neglect to inform their team of their deadlines. They meet the deadlines alright but submit mediocre work, not because they aren't good at the job but because they're spread too thin and haven't paid adequate attention to each task. Remember, 'excellence' is the word of the day. A company sometimes turns down opportunities, not because they can't do the job but because they know they can't do it to a high standard by the specified deadline. Also, they know they have a brand to protect. Companies that go under and start losing business do so because their customers lose faith in them. Treat yourself like the CEO of a company, and aim to maximise your brand, ensuring that sentiments attached to your brand include quality and excellence. Excellence must be one of your unique selling prepositions (USPs).

You must produce work that is better than that of the average intern. In essence, you are aiming to wow your team and exceed their expectations. Don't get intimidated and think you are not up to the task, you can do this. In fact, you are more than able – all it takes is preparing yourself day-to-day so that, on the day of reckoning, it would only be natural for you to excel. Remember that I am not writing this for students who are content with mediocrity, but for those who have decided that they will excel and achieve greatness. The key is to take gradual steps. I didn't start by writing a report assessing opportunities for my team or negotiating with directors in research companies on my first day. That was more towards the last quarter of my internship. I developed gradually. I said before that, it is better for the team to think you are on a certain level and then realise you are good than for them to think that you are very good and realise you are just good. Crawl before you walk. Too many interns are like babies who, having taken one step, suddenly try to run, and then they fall flat on their face under a pile of work they can't handle. This is simply because they haven't managed expectations properly.

Do It With A Smile

You can do an excellent job, and you can arrive early and leave last, but you also need to be fun to be around. You must be enthusiastic. I've seen interns get offers, not because they were the best technically, but because they were enthusiastic. That was the case for me; I always had a smile on my face. Granted, there were occasionally some down times when I felt I shouldn't have made a silly mistake or when I got told off, but I didn't let those times last for long. You see, when you are on a mission to succeed and you have a limited timeframe to prove yourself, you quickly realise that you don't have time to dwell on downtimes. You learn whatever lesson is necessary, and then keep on moving. Since I never said 'no' to work or frowned or dragged my feet when more work came my way, I became the 'go-to' person. I stayed late at work and gave it my all. I had accepted in my mind that 9-5 was the working day for the average person, but not for me, closing time was when the work was completed. So, you can take on more provided that you're willing to put in the hours. Your enthusiasm will even result in people willing to help you. During my internship in corporate banking, it was no secret that I wanted to work in investment banking, and my team did all they could to get me in there. It is difficult to be enthusiastic about what doesn't interest you. There was a clear difference between when I joined the bank and when I left. When I joined, I was excited to go to work. I loved working long hours and wanted to know everything about everything.

A year before I left, though, I had lost the zeal for work and had become bored. It was still busy, but I couldn't wait to leave each day. My line manager, at some point, asked where my enthusiasm had gone. I learnt a valuable lesson in that time; it is easier to flourish in an area that you're passionate about. If you are passionate about something, you will naturally be enthusiastic. So, discover your passion, but if you are unable to get into your choice industry at first, passionately serve where you are, and the fire in your heart for your dream job will over time, lead you to it. I often advise my mentees to organise at least one social event during the life of their internship, perhaps towards the middle of their internship, such as a night of bowling or karaoke. It is just a way of settling into the team and becoming one of the guys.

Celebrate Your Success

Overall success is made up of a series of successes. You must learn to celebrate each small success, as it is good for the soul and keeps your energy level up. For instance, I don't wait until I have finished a report before I consider it a success – writing the plan equals a pat on the back. Often, people get fed up when it seems like it is taking forever to get to the end of a task. As a result, their motivation level begins to drop, and the quality of the work suffers.

Keep the end in sight, but don't forget to enjoy the journey to the end. I have learnt to keep a running list of tasks, with all of the stages in each task delineated, and I cross out what I have done. A quick glance through all the tasks I've crossed out encourages me and keeps me going. In fact, I get a gift, a chocolate bar, a drink or whatever tickles my fancy at the time. Remember that those with a positive mental attitude become successful, and learn to look at things positively. For example, halfway through a project, some people would say that we have 50 percent of the work left to do, but I say that we have completed 50 percent, and knowing what we know now, we can do the rest of the project more quickly. If you don't celebrate the successes and appreciate your progress, then your work will quickly become a drag.

Knowledge

One of my favourite quotes by Dr Sola Fola-Alade is this: "Every leader is a reader." A leader simply means being the first in your internship and, eventually, in your field. If this is going to be you, then you must get accustomed to reading in general – about your field and work in particular. To be honest, this is why I wasn't number one; I wasn't a reader and I should have realised that you can't go further than you know. Read and learn something new every day, i.e. make every day count. What's interesting is that it isn't difficult. All it takes is discipline, and it certainly helps to be doing something you are passionate about.

As you cultivate your knowledge, remember to let everyone know of your progress. Make your knowledge known. You can do this by utilising what you are learning as a basis for conversations, simply stating what you learnt and asking someone's opinion on a particular point. I did this a lot during my internship and also as a graduate. Sometimes, when I felt cheeky, I would ask one colleague a question, and then later when speaking to another colleague, I'd bring it up as part of my knowledge bank and ask their opinion. You become a star in the eyes of your team when, in a team meeting, a question is asked that nobody can answer but you. So, know your stuff and show it in a subtle but clear manner.

If you are like me, you must leave those bad studying habits behind. You know what it was like in university – you study for an exam, but shortly afterwards, you forget it all. That won't work in the professional world. You want to learn and comprehend the entirety of the subject, inside and out. You want to know the reasons, whether there are alternatives, and all the pros and cons. It is certainly not as difficult as it sounds, and it actually becomes fun because you realise you are not learning only the subject, but other areas around it as well.

Be Humble And Do What's Needed

I remember when the MD had to let the secretary go and said to me that he couldn't replace her at the moment because of the credit crunch and that he expected me to take up some of her tasks. He said, "Uche, the secretary on Mark's team will help us with travel arrangements and stationery, but the team's invoices have to be done by someone on the team." At this point, he dropped a pile of invoices on my desk and said, "Please check with one of the other secretaries what process to follow." Confused, I thought to myself, "But I'm an investment banker. I've been in the bank for almost four years. He can't be serious." And despite these thoughts, I got up, took the pile of invoices and enthusiastically got to work. I didn't moan or protest that doing invoices was beneath me. I humbly went to a secretary and asked how to process invoices.

You see, there will be times when we will have to get our hands dirty doing work we wouldn't ordinarily do. I know you are in university and you are getting ready to embark on a high-flying career, but you will have your fair share of admin work, from photocopying to data processing and the list goes on. Even though you're being asked to do mind-numbing tasks, just get down to work and be diligent. You look very bad when you make mistakes on menial tasks like this, and being upset just makes it more likely that you will neglect to apply yourself. One partner in a consultancy firm decided to test how prepared an intern was for a permanent role, so he mischievously divided the internship into two halves – glory and gory. In the first half of the internship, he gave the intern exciting work to do. Obviously, the intern was ecstatic to be learning so much and be given such responsibility. She was very enthusiastic, performed well and learnt quickly. Then, halfway through, the partner changed from exciting work to huge amounts of data processing and photocopying, simply to see if the intern would remain enthusiastic and still want to learn. Surprisingly, the intern did remain upbeat and tried to learn everything about everything. Needless to say, she got the offer. It will take you far if you decide to enjoy yourself and maintain a good attitude during your internship regardless of the type of work you find yourself doing.

A man watched two labourers as they worked on a building. As he watched, he noticed that one of them kept groaning and cursing. When the man asked him what he was doing, he said, "I'm just putting one stone on top of another all day until my back gives in." Interestingly, the other one whistled and moved the stones swiftly in an enthusiastic manner. When he was asked what he was doing, he said, "Sir, I am not just building a wall, I'm building a cathedral." Adopting the attitude of the second labourer will give you an edge in your career.

Procrastination

Procrastination is one of the biggest enemies of success. "I will leave it till later," or even worse, "I will do it now but let it stretch out for as long as possible," or "I promise, tomorrow, I will start." Do those statements sound familiar? While you procrastinate, you will fail to maximise your potential. It is not a curse, it is just a fact. Procrastination is the thief of time; because tomorrow never comes and today is the tomorrow you were waiting for. The only cure is to change your thinking. Take out some blank sheets of paper and write this numerous times – 'DO IT NOW, DO IT NOW, DO IT NOW…' All procrastination does is give you temporary relief, but when you begin to connect it with a feeling of loss (i.e. missed opportunities), pain and regret, which is its inevitable result, you will break this habit and begin to handle tasks efficiently and as they arise. Even as you read, I am sure without any effort at all, you can think of multiple times when procrastination has cost you dearly. Please don't wait until you experience a big loss before you take heed of this advice. If you are going to succeed on your internship or any other endeavour, you must overcome the misled desire to procrastinate. On the issue of doing things quickly, please use this as a rule of thumb – if you have a list of things to do and there are some that will take just a few minutes to do, do them immediately. This not only allows you to cross a few things off of that lengthy list but it also gives you motivation to push on.

Gossiping

You might think, "Well, everyone does it," and you would be right to think that, but it is better to be different and stand out. If you behave like everybody else, you won't make it to the top. I always found it shocking to see a group of people gossiping about somebody and then when one person from the group would leave, they would start gossiping about the person who just left. What goes around comes around, though – if you gossip, you will be gossiped about even more. The seeds that we sow have a way of multiplying before the harvest. I don't gossip for several reasons; one, because I don't want to be gossiped about, and two, because I'm not perfect. So, if someone has a bad habit that is visible, I remind myself that I too have my own bad habits, and although they may not be visible, I don't want them spoken about. Wherever you are in life, gossiping is bad, but as an intern, you must not gossip, even if you are invited to. Don't even try it. I am not asking you to change the world and ensure that other people don't gossip, but you can change yourself. So, manage yourself and refrain from gossiping because it will save you a lot of hassle.

Chapter 10

More Key Success Factors For Your Transition

Mentors

Through mentoring, you can ensure that your diligence and hard work will have the biggest impact possible. Every successful person in any field has a mentor. You always need someone who has been where you're going and who can show you the best way to go about achieving your dream. I am both a mentor and a mentee and can confidently say that you are more likely to succeed if you have a mentor. It will also shorten your time of getting to the top. Mentors are there to save you time, money and the pain of learning from experience. They would tell you the truth that no one else wants to tell you and will encourage you to be better.

For example, one of my mentees in HSBC became so worked up on the job one day that she ended up crying in front of her colleagues. Now, as an intern, you are very unlikely to get a job offer after a crying episode because it indicates that you can't handle the pressure. She wanted to give up, but I spent time encouraging her and giving her tips on how she could redeem herself. By the end of the internship, she received an offer.

I remember on the day of my interview, a peer mentor briefly explained a particular finance concept he felt was important for me to know. At a point when the interview was slipping out of my hands, I explained the concept and the interviewers were visibly impressed. Boy, did that come in handy! Mentors are also useful when you want to ask questions that you feel uncertain about asking your manager and colleagues.

You can have both older and peer mentors. Older mentors often have less time and will be available less frequently, but after an hour with them, you will be changed, assuming you get it. Peer mentors, on the other hand, are your university buddies both in your year and years above. How do you get a peer mentor? Peer mentors are easy. Simply approach the students you admire and spend time building relationships with them. As for older mentors, you typically would be given a mentor when you start your career or you find one through networking. Build a relationship with them and then ask them to be your mentor.

Handling Mistakes

Even with the best will in the world, and being as careful as you can possibly be, you will still make mistakes. It's just a fact. Now, if you make mistakes on every task, then you are not paying adequate attention to your work and need to improve on your attention to detail. Are you a visual person or an auditory person? Do you "see" the other person's point of view or "hear" what they say? In other words, does it "look good" or "sound right"? Do you prefer to learn by listening or by reading? One way isn't better than the other. We each have what works best for us. In fact, trying to change this is like trying to get someone who is right-handed to write with their left hand. So, know what works for you. If you prefer to learn by listening, how about reading your report out loud to yourself? Hearing it out loud can make it easy for you to spot errors. Often, you can find a quiet spot in your office for this. If you work best by reading, then don't just read your work on screen – print it out and read it on paper too. Remember to pay attention to detail – check and re-check everything to make sure that no errors creep in. You can also ask your colleagues to cast an eye over it too; if one person misses something, another may spot it. While everyone makes mistakes, it is possible to minimise them.

So, what's the best way forward when you make mistakes like messing something up in a model or using the wrong database or leaving out important chunks of information? As with most things, it depends. Say, for instance, after submitting some work, you realise that you made a mistake. If you have enough time before it is sent out to a client, make your corrections and let your colleagues know. If you can't correct it in the time you have, then let your colleagues know quickly and make the correction. If the work has gone and there is nothing you can do about it, then, assuming it is a small mistake, you can take the chance of hoping no one will notice the mistake. If it is major though, don't dare ignore it hoping that no one will find out – alert your colleagues instead. You may get told off, but it is the responsible thing to do. Don't dwell on mistakes or internalise them. There is the job and then there is you as a separate entity. If a piece of work is bad, the work is bad and that does not mean you are bad at the job. That's how I have been able to survive; I never take it to heart. My work improved when I took the view that I am excellent at the job not because I deliver excellent work, but rather because I am excellent, I deliver excellent work. Begin to think along those lines: "As a man thinks in his heart, so is he."

Interestingly, one of the reasons interns tend to make mistakes is because they have this false mindset that someone will look over their work to catch the mistakes. This differentiates successful interns from unsuccessful ones. The successful intern knows that the buck stops with them, and they don't look to anybody to go over their work. They approach any given task as though it will be sent directly to the client. Now, most often, higher ups do review an intern's work, but with that sort of mindset, the quality of work they deliver is superb. If, in your mind, you believe that someone will go over your work, then the quality of your work will inevitably be lower. Take full responsibility, as though the head of your firm asked you to do it and your offer depends on it. Remember, overall success is a series of successes, and the buck stops with you.

We all have bad days at work – days when nothing seems to be going right or when it seems like you are making every possible mistake. During such times, it is important to remember that no matter how bad a day is going, there are only 24 hours in a day and it must come to an end. You must learn to balance the accounts at the end of each day – what went well, what went wrong, what could you have done differently or better. After the accounts are balanced and you've taken what you need from that day, let it go. The following morning, don't come in the same way you left the day before. It's a new day with new possibilities, and it could be your best day yet. Always remember that yesterday is the tomb, but tomorrow is in the womb. Yesterday has expired, but tomorrow can be inspired. Yesterday's mistakes or mishaps are only good for one thing – to learn from – but far too many workers let it dictate their today, tomorrow and future. Don't do that. Learn from each day all that it can teach you, but then make sure you let go.

Whilst we are on the topic of mistakes, let me highlight a golden rule you should adhere to when it comes to mobile phones. When you're at work, switch off your mobile phone. I know that sounds rather obvious and I am not saying that if you are found using your phone, it will negatively impact your chances of getting an offer. However, as I mentioned before, perception is everything, and frequent use of your mobile phone will give your colleagues the impression that you are not focusing on your work. Don't try to be disciplined by leaving your phone on and checking it once in a while. It is better to be safe rather than send out the wrong signal. My advice is that you should follow the golden rule and check your phone when you are going for lunch or having a short break. Also, unless your company has given you a phone to use during your internship don't take your mobile phone to any meetings.

People Are The Business

Being good with people is more important than technical ability when it comes to succeeding. This was confirmed by Stanford Research Institute, which reported that, out of the money we earn from our various endeavours, 12.5 percent depends on knowledge while 87.5 percent depends on our ability to deal with people. This is the reason why Teddy Roosevelt said, "The most important single ingredient to the formula of success is knowing how to get along with people." John D. Rockefeller said, "I will pay more for the ability to deal with people than any other ability under the sun." You can be a genius technically, but if you are not a people person and don't learn to be one, you will never make it to the top. You will have a job alright, but your progress will be limited.

It is said that, at the junior level, your technical ability is more important than your people skills, and I agree, but I have also learnt that the earlier you start developing your people skills, the better. For some, it comes naturally – they find it easy to strike up a conversation with anyone regardless of gender, race or age. If that's you, great, but take time to improve.

Any natural gift only becomes valuable when it is developed into a skill, and winning with people is one skill you must develop. I am naturally outgoing and friendly, but I realised that I found it easier to relate with people of a similar background (e.g., Africans), which is normal but certainly not enough. In university, I never really noticed this trend because I spent most of my time with friends from similar backgrounds. When I was working with other students on my course, the work at hand and the course material gave us a lot to talk about. Whilst at parties, though, most people were too drunk to make out what was being said. However, when I started working, I struggled with making small talk. After the traditional "Hi." and "How are you doing," I was blank, and I just prayed that the lift would come faster or someone would come to my rescue. I would also try to stay away from small groups of people who were talking. It was fine if it was people I knew well, but with new people, I worried about how I would look. What if I didn't have anything to say or said complete nonsense in this new circle? And as for senior people, I stayed clear, which was a sure way to cap my progress. To be honest, when I drilled down, it was an issue of confidence.

The beauty with life is that any and every skill can be learnt, if you decide to apply yourself. Once, at a success conference, the speaker said he was naturally very shy and reserved, but on realising the importance of relating with people and its role in his success, he read books like Dale Carnegie's *How to Win Friends and Influence People*. Now, that's what I call taking charge, and as you can imagine, I now have that book in my library. When it comes to people, you learn by doing. I had to change my thinking; for example, if I am speaking to someone and there is silence, that means that neither of us has anything to say, as opposed to me blaming myself for having nothing to say. I paid attention and observed the habits of those colleagues who I thought related well with people, and I realised that I had to stop trying so hard and simply let the conversation flow. Whatever question I am asked gives me something to say, and I can even throw the question back if I want. Furthermore, I am free to agree or disagree.

Being aware about what's going on in the world helps because that's what conversations are made of. With this new mindset, I stopped running and started engaging people more. If you are like I used to be, try stepping out of your comfort zone and make the most out of university by engaging people you otherwise would shy away from. Learn to make conversation and keep it going for a while. Read Dale Carnegie's book and as with any new skill, practice. Commit to talking with someone new each week. Remember, a smile is inviting. So, smile as much as you can, and let your energy be contagious. I can't stress how important it is to be enthusiastic and fun to be around. I had enough extra energy for my team to feed off, and in my reviews, it wasn't the quality of my work that got the most accolades, it was my diligence and enthusiasm.

In order to relate well with people, you must master the art of self-control and no, you are not always right. You can't afford to lose it simply because someone is getting on your nerves. Imprint the words "Don't snap," inside your head. Trust me, sometimes you will feel like rolling up your sleeves and punching someone, but never snap because if you do, all you're really proving is that you can't take the heat. Sometimes, people will intentionally push your buttons, but just let it go. Step away from the desk and get some fresh air. I used to go call my girlfriend or one of my other friends and scream down the phone. After I had calmed down, I went back to my desk and kept at it. Someone told me the story of a four-year-old who was being naughty one evening, so his mum reprimanded him and told him to go and sit down in the corner as punishment. Our little chap walked over to the chair, sat down, and said, "Mum, I am sitting on the outside, but I am standing on the inside." Often, I will be fuming on the inside, but on the outside I would be calm. When I was younger, I used to think I was tough if I told people off and said exactly how I felt. I was proud of it. I thought, "That's how I am, take it or leave it." Now, I realise I was immature, and such an attitude does not work in the professional world. Thankfully, I saw the light early on and changed my ways.

Feedback

Never rely on how well you think you're doing; always actively seek feedback from your team. I am not suggesting that you ask for feedback every day. Allow a couple of weeks to pass, so your team can get a feel for what you're made of, and then ask for feedback. Don't let your midterm review be the first time you receive feedback from your team – that's too late.

When you ask for feedback on your midterm review, be prepared to give a summary of how you think you're doing. This is an opportunity to highlight key successes, how much you have learnt, what you think you need to improve on and how much you are enjoying yourself. Ensure you maximise the opportunity. Whenever I asked for feedback, I always said that I was keen on knowing what I could improve and asked for advice on how to do so. Now, that wasn't so that I could look keen, but so I could actually improve.

At the midterm review stage, make sure to ask whether you're on track to getting an offer, and ask what you need to do more of in order to increase the likelihood that you receive an offer within the time you have left. You want to leave the meeting room with a plan for how you can work on your development points, and your manager should be happy to help. And if you receive negative feedback, don't get emotional. Take it with a smile and use it to your advantage. Your reaction to their feedback is actually a chance to give your team one more box to put a "well done'" tick in. Always remember that, like you, your manager and senior executives also receive feedback and development points, so never take it personally – you are not being victimised. The good feedback works the same way. You have to keep up the good work and ensure the boxes for those good remarks remain ticked at the end. Always remember that it is better to improve than to let a rating slip from positive to negative.

Nothing Beats A Power Nap

As we discussed before, sleeping on the desk is a sure way to kiss your offer goodbye. So, what do you do when you are tired and can't go on, as this will certainly be the case at times. Obviously, you can get some coffee, take a walk, wash your face and the list goes on. These options work, but there are some times when you are simply too tired and none of these options will do the trick. Like everybody else, I had gotten hooked on coffee, but at some point, I got sick of it and just didn't like the idea of being addicted to anything, so I found what works for me. I decided to give my body what it needed – sleep.

So, when I was tired, on my lunch break, I would go to one of the floors higher up, find a quiet spot where no one could see me, and have a power nap for fifteen to twenty minutes. I highly recommend it. It is the most refreshing experience. Now, if you ever try this, make sure you take your phone and set an alarm or you might end up being woken up by the night crew! I always held my phone in hand so I could feel it vibrate. As you can see, I had it all figured out. I am certain a lot of people did exactly the same thing, but I did not dare not tell anyone what I was doing, even as a joke. In my opinion, companies should encourage their people to take power naps. After all, research shows that it restores alertness and enhances performance. It has been statistically proven that power naps (e.g. a 40-minute nap) improves performance by 34 percent and alertness by 100 percent.

Interestingly, many of the great people whom we emulate are known to have taken regular power naps, including Winston Churchill, JF Kennedy, Albert Einstein and Thomas Edison.

Chapter 11

The Awesome Four:
Strategies For Success

Steve

By the end of his internship, Steve was smooth sailing. He had completed two different five-week rotations and had made his mark in both. Earlier on during the internship, he decided to get in first and leave last. He couldn't figure out why any interns would leave early and risk implying that they had nothing to do or had learnt all they could. He recalls that, initially, he had nothing to do, apart from getting coffee, but since he worked on a desk that traded around 70 bonds, he decided to learn everything he could about these bonds. Then, something interesting happened. The more he read, the more questions he asked; and the more questions he asked, the more responsibilities he was given. Often, someone would say, "You know, the question you asked ... do this, and it will help you understand it better." That was how he started getting more than coffee orders to do.

His team was impressed because he was receptive to learning. They were excited to have somebody they could mould, as opposed to someone who had his own ideas of how things should be. To crown it all up, of his own accord, he created a model that would tell his team which bond would be profitable if there was a significant shift in the market, such as a takeover. Just so we are clear, that is the sort of task an associate does. It was no surprise that, at the end of his first rotation, his MD asked him to write his own review and then simply signed it. In his second rotation, he simply applied his winning formula – being the first in and last out, being inquisitive and genuinely wanting to learn, treating each responsibility like it was his last opportunity, and doing all he could to add value.

As expected, Steve received an offer and gladly accepted it. Being a doctor was now out of the question. He enjoyed himself and decided this was his new path. By the time he started his analyst programme, there was a credit crunch, and he had to relive his intern days, hoping for a job after each of his three rotations. During his first rotation on a Wednesday, he came into work and five people from his seven member team had been fired. With the MD who had promised him a job offer gone, Steve was back to square one. At the end of his second rotation, although his team were impressed with him, they were downsizing, so he had little hope of getting a permanent job there. He had only one more chance to secure a job after his third rotation. If he did not get a job after his third rotation, that would be it – he would be back in the job market. Like me, he had six months to prove himself.

By the end of the rotation, he had surpassed his team's expectations, but then the last blow came when his team's headcount was pulled, and he realised that they wouldn't be able to offer him a job. In three weeks, his rotation would be over and he had no job offer. His boss, upset that his star analyst was going to be leaving, went to his colleague in another team that was hiring and told him about Steve. There was only one issue, though – his colleague had four analysts to choose from, all of whom had spent six months on his desk. As a gesture of good faith, he agreed for Steve to spend a week on his desk, and at the end of the week, he would decide between Steve and the other four analysts. Steve had nothing to lose; all he could do was work hard and try to make his mark in a week. This would be the shortest internship he ever heard of. By the end of the week, the MD did something interesting – he asked his team members to cast a vote on which analyst they wanted to keep. To each analyst's surprise, most of the team chose him. They saw his determination. The MD told him, "We were very impressed that although you had only one week and we expected you to assume it was a lost cause, you gave it your all, really believing the impossible – that you could get an offer. Most importantly, you get along very well with the guys."

As I have said time and time again, it isn't over until it's over.

Fatima

To Hussein, Fatima was a good mentee who knew little but wanted to learn. To her team, she was an intern who learnt quickly and was keen on getting a job. Fatima's secret was to get as many tips from her mentor as possible and to do what he suggested. Hussein made it quite clear that being shy and timid wouldn't cut it, so she needed to snap out of it. She then told her manager she wanted to get a job and asked what her manager would like to see her achieve in the next ten weeks for that to happen. Her manager was impressed and told her she liked the fact that she was tough, which she needed to be in order to survive in the industry.

Thomas the knowledgeable intern had become inconsequential to her. She stopped letting his way of showing off get to her. Besides, she looked more teachable, so the difference became a plus. Fatima constantly played the "Let me do that for you, so that you can focus on more important things." card or the "If you need to go, is there something I can finish up for you?" card, and her team thought she was heaven on earth. Yes, it won her many late nights, but what was she there for anyway? Towards the end of her internship, another tip from Hussein came in useful – first she ensured that she had a properly detailed account of how she had met each of her manager's criteria for success, and then she asked her manager for a chat. Not intending to show off, she reiterated how deeply she wanted an offer, and she recapped all that she had done to meet and surpass the criteria. On that faithful last day, her manager called her into a meeting room and gave her the good news.

Unlike most other students, Fatima wasn't completely convinced that banking was the best way to start her career in finance. She applied to a few accounting firms, including the one that had rejected her previously, but this time – with an offer in hand and HSBC on her CV – they wanted to talk. She got a place with EY and wondered whether it was smarter for her to get professional qualifications early in her career or do banking. EY really wanted her, so they agreed to defer her offer for one year, during which time she joined HSBC. By the end of the year, she had decided that she could always come back to banking, and told HR she was leaving. However, by this time, Fatima had become a star. She had earned exceptionally good ratings in her two rotations and was being featured on HSBC's website. After much deliberation, she decided to leave, and is now a fast-rising star in EY. Compare where Fatima was and where she is now. Doesn't that prove that only you can stop you?

Leke

Leke worked hard at correcting the mistakes he made early on, and he managed to impress his team by mastering the pricing that he muddled up before. His visible frustration about messing up showed that he wasn't used to failing. After giving higher priority to an associate's work over that of a VP, he learnt his lesson and never said no again. Whenever a similar situation came up, he let his colleagues decide which piece of work was more important. He too left his mark – he created a model that automated certain tasks on his team; and for this, he received accolades.

Towards the end of the internship, two things had become evident – firstly, that he could do the job well and secondly, that he wasn't passionate about it. That was where he differed from Steve. He had an interest, but he lacked the genuine passion. As the passion question had come up a couple of times, he knew he wouldn't be getting the offer. On his last day, his MD told him, "You're a smart guy and the most professional in our intern class, but I just think the bank culture isn't for you. In a place where self-promotion is the norm, you are quiet." He continued, "I am very happy to give you a good reference if you need it, though, and one final point – your approach to most tasks shows you are more of a consultant than a banker." That last statement was all Leke needed to hear. Now, he was clear that consultancy was the way. Six years later, Leke is now the European Service Director for a mid-cap consultancy firm. In those six years, he has had to deal with a redundancy and one failed investment vehicle, but he is still strong and pushing forward. Only you can stop you.

Matilda

Matilda decided to play it safe, like I said, so there was little room for error, but there was also little room to impress, particularly in just two weeks. She spoke only when spoken to and tried not to step on anyone's toes. She did what she was told and nothing more. In hindsight, she says she could have been more proactive. She said that she always thought about other ways of doing each task and wondered why they couldn't be done differently, but not wanting to ask any stupid questions, she kept her thoughts to herself. Also, she acknowledged she could have been friendlier in comparison to the other interns. She didn't make much of an effort to build relationships because she thought, "What's the point ... I'll be gone in two weeks." She certainly didn't have the mindset of being a graduate taking a year out to study; she was very much an intern and acted like one. Matilda didn't get the offer, but she was invited for a few interviews with a magic circle law firm, and this time, she knew what they wanted to see in an application. Her internship played a big part in getting these interviews. She was soon offered a place with Norton Rose, and now is an associate.

End

Towards the end of your internship, your fate is likely to have already been decided, so your aim is to ensure that there are no last-minute mess-ups. Ironically, although you have spent the whole summer trying to prove yourself, everything can be ruined in a single moment. If you've been shining throughout and delivering excellent work, then it's unlikely that a mistake will cause your team and HR to change their mind. It's the more significant issues, though – going overboard with your drinking, snapping at a team mate or just getting too complacent – that can cause your offer to evaporate. The motto "It ain't over 'til it's over" also applies to not messing up your chances.

An occurrence in an American football game, years ago, helps to illustrate this point. Coach Bryant's University of Alabama football team were winning by six points with just two minutes left in the final quarter. He gave his quarterback simple instructions to play it safe and run out the clock, but the quarterback, full of adrenaline, had his own ideas. He went to his team and said, "Coach wants us to play it safe, but as you know, they'll be expecting that; instead, let's surprise them with a pass play." When the quarterback received the ball, he threw it, and it was intercepted by a defending cornerback who happened to be a champion sprinter. As the cornerback headed for a touchdown, the quarterback, who was known to be an average runner, suddenly ran with the speed of light towards the cornerback and, to everyone's surprise, tackled him from behind with five yards to go, saving the game. Once the game was over, the other coach asked Coach Bryant, "I thought your quarterback was an average runner, how did he run down my speed star?" Coach Bryant said smiling, "Your man was running for six points, mine was running for his life!"

So, unless you're willing to do the impossible and save the game at the very end, just play it safe. You want to finish strong, and my advice is to finish stronger than you started. By this time, you should be seen as a team member who is about to go on a one-year sabbatical. As such, spend time tying up loose ends, be it finalising the work you have done, saving documents you have been working on in the right places (i.e. where they can be found by others on your team) or going for coffee with key individuals in your new network.

Redefining 'Success' On An Internship

When I did my internship, 'success' simply meant getting the job offer.

But now, I like to see the offer as the icing on the cake. While getting an offer should be your main focus, don't lose sight of the fact that your internship is a valuable opportunity to learn and build a solid network. If you didn't get an offer, your CV has greatly improved and you are now better placed than a lot of students. It is always good to put things in perspective because everything depends on how you look at it. Some see rejection as a loss, while others see it as the dawning of a new opportunity. This reminds me of a story about two buckets. On the way to the stream, this one bucket always complained about being empty on its way back to the stream. "Oh, how miserable I am," it cried. However, the second bucket was excited that it went to the stream empty, but came back full, "Oh, how great it is to be useful," it shouted. One type of intern cries and mopes that he didn't get an offer. Then, there is the other type of intern, who, despite that disappointment, is thrilled at the opportunity that he has had and looks to the bright future that he eagerly awaits.

There are many examples of individuals who did not receive an offer from the team where they worked but were offered multiple offers from competitors. Sometimes, it could be that the culture of the bank or firm is just not for you or your team is not hiring; so if an offer does not come through, that certainly is not the end of the world. In fact, you're still very well placed to get your dream job, even if it is with another company. Your attitude is what determines how effective you will be in landing your job.

Celina, a friend of mine who did her internship in the same year as I did, was patient as we both eagerly awaited our job offers – me from HSBC and her from Lehman Brothers. The day I got mine, I did everything I could to avoid seeing her, because I didn't know how she would take it. However, in the evening, when I ran into her, and my grinning gave it away. She said, "What's up, Uche? What's all the smiling about?" Trying to make it seem like I was only a bit happy, I said, "I didn't get into investment banking, but I got into corporate banking." To my surprise, she was very excited too and said she would be joining the list of those who had offers soon.

Lehman Brothers did not make her an offer, but with her great attitude, it was only a matter of time before she would get her offer. By the end of our final year, she still had no offer, and by now, everyone in the crew was heading off to banks, law, and accounting and consultancy firms. She was unable to rectify her mess-up in her second year and finished with a 2.2. When I heard about her GPA, even I, optimistic Uche, thought there was no hope. The best she could do was to do a Master's, get a distinction and hopefully be offered something afterwards. Celina thanked me for my advice, but kept applying, and in the meantime, signed up for a course to improve her computer skills. Utilising the network that she had created during her internship, she was able to get an interview for another internship in a different bank. She was interviewing with students who were a year below her and who had not done an internship, so she was one of the best candidates and was offered a place. Learning from the mistakes, she had made in her first internship, and having the benefit of greater experience, she set herself apart from the other interns and became the talk of the intern class. The norm would have been for her to get an offer, return to university perhaps to do a Master's degree and start work the following year; however, by the end of her internship, her team were so impressed with her performance that they bent the rules so that she could start immediately as an analyst. When you are excellent, the rules can change, like they did for myself and Celina. What is most interesting is that, a few years later, when banks were laying off staff in the credit crunch, Celina was being promoted. As I said earlier, it isn't how you start, but how you finish, that really matters.

Being on an internship does not necessarily mean you will get a job with that company. You may find that the company is not for you and you may even decline their offer. That is what happened with Hadiza, a woman I interned with at HSBC. She was a whiz kid, who was well suited for the research division, and there was no doubt in anybody's mind that she would have been excellent; however, she decided to work as an economist for a development agency. She turned down the offer and did a Master's degree at

Oxford instead. I then heard that she was working with the World Bank as an economist.

Then there was Andrew, a guy on my graduate programme who, like everybody else, was excited to be starting his career. Six months into working, he decided that it wasn't what he had in mind. Unlike me, he hadn't done an internship and didn't know exactly what he was getting into. Everyone tried to convince him to stay and try out other areas in the bank, but he decided to leave and try out another career. Unlike Hadiza and Andrew, many students try hard to succeed at that which they are not cut out for, rather than bite the bullet and seek out what will make them happy. Eventually, they end up being unhappy and even sacked. One of the key aims of an internship is to assess whether your dream job is for you, and if you find out that it isn't, then you have to be brave enough to give it up and look for something you're passionate about. Once you find that, you will feel naturally compelled to apply yourself and give everything you've got.

What Next?

It might seem strange for me to ask this question after I spent the whole book talking about how to succeed in your internship and career, but sometimes things don't work out the way we intend them to. Life isn't always fair, but what do we do when we have done our best and still have not achieved our dream or goal? Yogi Berra says, "You give 100 percent in the first half of the game, and if that isn't enough, in the second half, you give what is left." That attitude demonstrates why Yogi was one of only four baseball players to be named MVP of the American league three times, and was also elected to the Baseball Hall of Fame. I always say that it isn't over until you get what you want. So, if at first, you don't get your ideal job, keep trying; but in the meantime, start with what you have.

My friend Yinka is a good example of someone who simply would not take no for an answer or settle for anything less than his dream. He realised that if he gave up on his dream once, giving up other aspirations would continue to be an option when things did not go as planned, and he was not about to let that happen. Yinka had finished with AAA in A Levels, went to Cambridge and finished with a 2.1 in Chemical Engineering. He was also featured on BBC2's Black Ambition TV series, which tracked up-and-coming stars during their university life. His dream was to become a trader, and with his stellar track record and achievements, you would have expected him to have his pick of which bank he wanted to work for and what trading desk he wanted to start with. Yinka tried hard to get into trading, but was unlucky time and time again. Like any other graduate, he needed a job, and since trading was not forthcoming, he started in the operations division at one of the investment banks. He was faithful in this role and spent the next two years within the operations division, always knowing in his mind that trading was his goal. During this time, he networked with traders, continued learning and gradually started making his interest known. On his own and without the support of his manager, who selfishly did not want to lose Yinka's talent, he tried to get into trading. On the way, he encountered many excuses, but because of his persistence, he was offered an interview within the trading division at his bank. What was meant to be a couple of interviews turned out to be 15 interviews, at the end of which he was told, "Sorry, we think you're best suited for operations." At this point, he was very angry. We all knew it was easier to move divisions within your bank than trying to move to another bank, particularly if you were trying to move from back office to front office. What was he going to do?

I thought he would forget the dream, but he didn't. He started to look elsewhere, knowing his chances were slim. He was offered an interview with another investment bank to do trading, and after a while, they offered him a place, but he would have to start as a graduate alongside individuals who had just finished university, even though he had left Cambridge two years prior to this offer. He would have to take a pay cut and become the most junior person on the team again. I couldn't believe it when he told me he was going to take it. He said, "Uche, I want to be a trader, that's my dream, and if, to move ahead, I have to stoop to conquer, then that's what it's going to be. Besides, I will have six months to burn, so I can fulfil my dream of learning Spanish. I will head to Spain for six months and enrol in a school." Impressed, I told him he would be an awesome trader with such determination and belief. He took the job, and so began his trading career; he gave it his best shot and was having the time of his life.

Towards the end of his graduate programme, he encountered problems with a couple of senior people on the team, and they advised him to take a job in another part of the bank. In essence, they were saying, "We don't think you'll make it in trading, at least not in this bank." Seeing no point in fighting these senior guys, he decided it was time to leave, and when I asked him "What next?" he said, "Well, another trading role is my aim, just not here." He had been there before and was not going let anyone tell him what he could or could not do, so he started applying and got an interview with HSBC, this time, for a manager role, which would mean a double promotion and close to twice his current pay. He did not think he would get it because he clearly did not have the experience, but to his surprise, HSBC wanted him. They thought his Goldman experience was what they needed, plus his Spanish would come in handy because the person who was in charge of Spanish contracts needed to shed some clients. In all honesty, I was shocked – here was a guy with a dream who simply would not give up. He was a wonder in HSBC, making money for the bank, and as well as earning twice as much, he was given a guaranteed bonus. Yinka continues to be a source of inspiration to many who have a dream and have decided to keep at it, even though things have not started off as they would have liked. So, if you did not get what you wanted, then what next? Keep learning and practicing, and in the meantime, start with what you have.

Epilogue

Comparing where I am now to the place that I came from, I would have laughed in the face of anyone who told me I would excel in investment banking. If you read on a piece of paper that I was promoted on trial to year 9, barely passed O Levels with C's and a couple of B's and that I barely got the grades I needed to get into Bristol, you probably wouldn't think that I'd get into investment banking. However, like many others, I have proved that if you make up your mind and decide to apply yourself, then nothing can stop you. Remember that if the "Mind of a man can conceive and believe it, he can achieve it." By reading this book, you are an individual who has the potential to be one of the movers and shakers in their field and in their generation, but that potential will remain as just potential unless vision, belief, determination and action are introduced into the equation. Dr Myles Munroe says that the wealthiest places in the world aren't the diamond mines of South Africa or the oil fields in the Middle East, but rather the graveyards where individuals with dreams and potential died without maximising their potential or fulfilling their dream.

Whether or not you succeed and maximise your potential is up to you and no one else. Little by little is the way to go, successful people know that time is finite, and they have mastered the art of numbering their days. They make each day count, ensuring that it pays tribute to the goal ahead. Thirty minutes to an hour of daily reading and practice will set you apart from the pack and cause you to outshine others in interviews, in your internship and your career.

Contentment is a good thing, but do not be content with mediocrity. Therefore, I implore you to dream big and take time to visualise daily where you want to work and what you ultimately want to become. Then, begin to take the daily steps necessary to manifest the future that you envision. Allow no place in your mind for thoughts about giving up, and what was once a dream will slowly but surely become real. You are a star in the making, and nothing can stop you but you. There is no obstacle you will come across that isn't common to man; so, don't be a quitter, but rather view each obstacle as an opportunity to grow stronger and gain insight. The truth to success remains the same all over the world – your life is only a reflection of who you think you are and what you believe you can achieve. Diligence is the bridge between your vision and your future reality, and the prize belongs to those who hang in there until they achieve their dream. Obstacles are valuable because they test how badly you want what you want, and passion and enthusiasm are what makes the journey of life enjoyable and worthwhile.

I could write another page full of examples of individuals who have done great things, but instead, I will simply state for one last time the one truth that helped them achieve such greatness. Your success in your interviews, your internships and your life ultimately depends on you and no one else. The truth is this – **ONLY YOU CAN STOP YOU**. There is one quality that you must possess in order to win, this is, as Napoleon Hill described it, "definiteness of purpose, the knowledge of what one wants and a burning desire to possess it."

Lightning Source UK Ltd.
Milton Keynes UK
UKOW08f2030040517
300514UK00001B/1/P